D1490888

That's Just
How My

Spirit
Travels

Rosemary in 1962 in her yellow raincoat ("my favorite photo").

# That's Just How My Spirit Travels

~ A Memoir

## Rosemary Fillmore Rhea

**unity**®
HOUSE
Unity Village, Missouri

3  3210  1168604

First Edition 2003

Copyright © 2003 by Rosemary Fillmore Rhea. All rights reserved. No part of this book may be used or reproduced in any manner whatsoever without written permission from Unity except in the case of brief quotations embodied in critical articles and reviews or in the newsletters and lesson plans of licensed Unity teachers and ministers. For information, address Unity House, 1901 NW Blue Parkway, Unity Village, MO 64065-0001.

To receive a catalog of all Unity publications (books, cassettes, compact discs, and magazines) or to place an order, call the Customer Service Department: 1-800-669-0282.

The publisher wishes to acknowledge the editorial work of Michael Maday and Raymond Teague; the copy services of Kay Thomure, Marlene Barry, and Jenny Leckbee; and the marketing efforts of Kim West, Wendy Rumsey, and Sharon Sartin.

On the cover: Rosemary at "check-point Charlie" in Berlin in 1961.

Cover photography by Reza Badiyia

Cover and interior design by Karen Rizzo

The New Revised Standard Version is used for all Bible verses, unless otherwise stated.

Library of Congress Control Number: 2003101748

ISBN 0-87159-286-X

Canada BN 13252 9033 RT

Unity House feels a sacred trust to be a healing presence in the world. By printing with biodegradable soybean ink on recycled paper, we believe we are doing our part to be wise stewards of our Earth's resources.

Dedicated to my children,
Rosalind and Rick,
who have shared much of my journey
and have been my life's greatest blessings
and
to all those amazing people
who were a part of creating that
lovely, magical place called Unity Farm.

Rosalind, Rosemary, and Rick Grace near the Bridge of Faith at Unity Village in the 1950s.

# Acknowledgments

This book could not have been printed without the help of dear friends who somehow deciphered my handwriting and typed it into their computers. It was not an easy task. I shall forever be grateful to Lorna Cheong and Dennis Meadows in Jamaica and to Debbie Ball and Vickie Nelson in America.

I want to give thanks to my dear friend Jane Truax for invaluable assistance in editing this book and preparing it to give to the publisher and to Karon Shewmaker who has helped in so many ways.

I would also like to pay tribute to beautiful Sylvia Teague, who helped so much with her suggestions and comments in the beginning; I pray that she knows the book has finally been completed.

# Table of Contents

# Foreword

*By Michael A. Maday*

Rosemary is back in Jamaica. In fact, she called me yesterday morning from Kansas City's airport, wanting to check on another detail on her book, but by now I'm sure she's settled back into Jamaica's intriguing ways.

You can feel a rhythm moving in this book. Most of it comes from Rosemary Fillmore Rhea herself, her natural spirit, her humility, her quiet wisdom, her quick wit, her determination to make sure her opinion is heard. Some of it is what Rosemary calls the "pulse of Jamaica," the culture, the climate, and a subterranean stream of mysticism that runs through the island.

Almost all of this book was written in Jamaica in between numerous forays back to the Mainland, mainly Unity Village here in the Heartland. Rosemary is loved wherever her spirit takes her, and you'll soon know why firsthand. The granddaughter of Unity's cofounders Charles and Myrtle Fillmore, she carries with her a strong sense of their pioneering spirit, and so to spend a little time with Rosemary brings a knowing of how Unity came into being and how it grew into what it is today.

It has been my privilege to get to know Rosemary during the developmental and substantive edits of this book. I want to say that I am deeply honored that she wanted me, from all her possible choices, to write this Foreword.

So let me say this book is not a history of Unity; there have been a number of those, especially Neal Vahle's recent (and excellent) *The Unity Movement*, that will give you detail and sequence. This is a memoir, a loving and personal story of one woman's life and her love of a place and of a movement that shaped her and so many others.

Rosemary Fillmore Grace Rhea is now a very different person than the girl and young woman who began her journey back when Unity Village was a farm and headquarters was in Kansas City. This book does an excellent job of creating the feeling of what it was like growing up here and being part of the formative—and in many ways the most prosperous—years of Unity's growth. There have been many "lead changes" here: many persons have come and gone, and as her story will show, many have been colorful and even famous! Running throughout her story, however, is a golden thread, similar to Jamaica's underground stream, that is a kind of precious energy which is as close to Rosemary as her own heartbeat, what she would call her heritage.

When she came back from her incredible adventure of touring the world back in 1962, as you'll read about in the pages ahead, she received a fair dose of criticism from people offended by her acceptance of other religions and other cultures. For me, she reveals her true colors here and shows Unity at its very best when she realizes that other people have not had the benefit of growing up at Unity Farm with her family and the extended family of Unity workers, so they don't have the benefit of a larger outlook.

It is that outlook which best exemplifies the Unity movement, the movement which tries to leave no one out, which literally tries to follow the teachings and example of Jesus Christ and love one another. And Rosemary doesn't shirk her responsibility of acknowledging where Unity has fallen short of this standard, especially where people of color are concerned, and you'll read about that as well.

At the end of this memoir, you'll see a section called Notes. More than a depository of references, it also contains some amusing anecdotes and insightful quotations that enhance the text—so don't pass it by! And you'll want to read the Appendix, the beautiful "Stella Maris" (which originally was an audiocassette that Rosemary wrote and the School produced in the late '70s), that complements this book so well.

Unity is at a crossroad. We are starting a new century and a new millennium, and for the first time, the Fillmore family is no longer running the day-to-day organization. This presents many opportunities and many challenges, as Rosemary suggests in her final chapter.

Always a pioneer, first in broadcast journalism on radio and television; recognized in *Who's Who of American Women*; and now an advisor to the movement of Global New Thought, Rosemary expects great things from Unity in the years to come.

She, like other members of her remarkable family, has that incredible ability to face adversity and see the beginnings of a whole new way of living. Life is perceived as an adventure and meant to be lived that way. No doubt, that is why Rosemary extols the virtues of Jamaica—the way her people smile in spite of their poverty and the way her spirit calms anxiety, heals the wounded soul, and springs up bright-eyed ready to begin again.

Unity Village, Missouri
December 2002

Michael A. Maday is editor of Unity House and consulting editor of *Unity Magazine*. An ordained Unity minister, he served as anthologist and writer for *New Thought for a New Millennium*, to which Rosemary Rhea also contributed.

# Sea Star and Soft Winds

## Sea Star—1997

We arrived after a long drive through tropical forests, interrupted only occasionally by small villages. He knew where we were going. Together we had decided on an island retreat. Neither one of us could remember exactly why we had chosen Jamaica, but once we did, he went before me to find a home for us to share for a while so that we both might write free from people and places that demanded attention.

I trusted his judgment. I knew he would choose the right place for what we needed to accomplish. Our friendship encompassed many years. We had similar interests, and both of us found solace and inspiration by the sea. However, nothing had prepared me for the beauty of the place he had found.

How can I describe it? The house itself is white, but it is surrounded by clear turquoise sea. The sun reflecting on the ocean shines softly throughout the house. Every room has vases filled with tropical flowers; it is as if a garden is blooming in every corner.

Not far from shore, waves slide gently over a shallow reef. The house is open to the sea, so you are continuously embraced by the movement of the breeze against your cheeks, and your body is lulled into relaxed submission by the constant movement of the changing tides. Every house on the island has a name. This one is called "Sea Star." And whoever named it must have lain on a bed, as I did last night, and observed the galaxy of the heavens merging with the ocean to form a cosmic whole.

If you doubt the mystery of the invisible, I must tell you this. Many, many years ago, when I needed a time away from the turbulence that was pushing me out of one phase of life into another, I was led to another house by the sea. It was a continent away from this island, by a different ocean with a less tranquil surf. But it was the right place for me at that time, for I was far from tranquil. The pounding, changing surf reflected the emotions that were sweeping through me.

The place I found so many years ago also had a name. It was called "Stella Maris"—Latin for "Star of the Sea." I lived in that house by the sea for twelve months. The sea calmed my anxious thoughts and healed my wounded spirit. When it was time for me to leave Stella Maris, I was ready to begin again.

Many years have passed now, and I'm a much different person than the young woman who spent that year at Stella Maris. People whom I loved have come and gone. There has been joy, and there has been pain. The years have taught me that we are on a journey, and if we trust God's travel plan, it will lead us safely through all the twists and turns that are a part of the human experience.

One of the nicest parts of growing older is the realization that those events that seemed so threatening when I was younger were essential to my growth and unfoldment. As I have moved through the years, I have begun to see that things *do* work out and time *does* heal, and although change is the very essence of life, there is a strong thread that is continuously weaving the fabric of our lives. If we stray too far from the grand design, we will be pulled back.

Here at Sea Star there are three staff members—Miss Pearl, Cherry, and Devon. They are gentle, warm people who have lived their lives on the island. And much of why Sea Star is so special, so unique, is the spirit that expresses itself through them. Yesterday Devon took me out in his canoe. He wanted me to see a small island offshore, a place where snorkeling is especially good. Devon is thirty-four years old, although he looks much younger. As he paddled quietly through the clear water, I asked him if he was happy.

He seemed surprised by the question. "Yes," he answered, "I am happy." However, I pursued the question: "Do you feel that anything is missing in your life—do you have dreams of things that you would like to do?"

He thought for a moment and then smiled and answered: "Oh, yes, I would like to travel. Sometimes I dream of working in the United States or England, but my life is good here and right now I'm happy."

I couldn't help but think of the young people I know at home who are his age. Most are trying to fit career, children, and the pursuit of happiness into one day, while still having time for a visit to their therapist. Devon is one of eleven children. He is second to the youngest. If he suffers from lack of parental love or sibling rivalry, he hides it well. *Webster* defines *happy* as being lucky or fortunate. So I asked myself, "Who is the lucky one—the fortunate one—Devon or someone living the so-called 'good life' in our competitive Western society?" The answer is, of course, individualistic. What would make me happy would not necessarily be happiness for you.

Real lasting happiness, it seems to me, is the ability to find joy in what you are doing with whomever you are doing it. The most truly joyous person I have ever known was my grandfather, Charles Fillmore. He achieved a level of happiness that few enjoy. When I knew him he was in the latter part of his life, but he had maintained a childlike enthusiasm for living. Life for him was a grand adventure, and children as well as adults were drawn to him like a magnet.

My grandfather was not an ordinary man; he was one of the enlightened ones. There are times when a person comes into the world with a special message for humankind. We call these people prophets, mystics. While they are with us, we are inspired not only by their message but also by the consciousness of love and joy that radiates through them. My grandfather was one of these people.

But what about the rest of us who are still driven by our emotions and desires? Our moments of happiness come and go with the shifting winds of circumstance. For instance, my friend who found Sea Star is now frustrated by the very things that drew us here. The peace and tranquility that soothe my mind have for him become boring and uninteresting. He thrives on action; he needs places to go and things to do. Each day he spends more and more time on the phone talking with his business partner in the States. Our reason for coming to Jamaica doesn't seem to be working. For different reasons both of us are experiencing difficulties with our writing. He is caught up with what is happening at home and the excitement he is missing, while I am so wrapped in my surroundings that my incentive to do much of anything floats away in the gentle breeze.

I have discovered that there is a mysticism running like a subterranean stream through the island, and occasionally, when you least expect it, it surfaces and surprises you with its strength and clarity. In the daytime the pulse of Jamaica is slow and deliberate, but as the sun goes down the rhythm changes and the sounds of reggae, calypso, and the songs of spiritual revival echo throughout the land. As I said, the spirit of Jamaica is reflected in its people. Jamaicans are passionate and caring, and regardless of the difficulties they experience, they somehow are still able to laugh and love. Life here is not easy. There is high inflation, few jobs, and extremely low wages, and yet most people manage to maintain a positive attitude. Jamaicans are also deeply religious: there are more churches per capita here than anywhere else in the world.

I asked a Jamaican friend who manages a local bank how people live with so little money and such high inflation. "Magic," he answered. "Magic." There is no other way to logically explain it. Bob Marley, who was the voice of Jamaica, sang, "There is a natural mystic blowing through the wind." And it is my guess that it is this innate spirituality that gives Jamaicans the power not only to survive but to survive with dignity and courage.

Visitors to the island fall into two categories: those who love it and those who feel no affinity with it and can't leave fast enough. Many writers and artists have found Jamaica so appealing that they built homes on the island. Writer Ian Fleming, of the James Bond books, composer Oscar Hammerstein, and actors Noel Coward and Errol Flynn are just a few of those who have found inspiration here. In the '40s and '50s, it was considered by the rich and famous the place to go in season. But after Jamaica gained its independence in 1962, the powerful elite began seeking new sanctuaries for their winter solace.

However, tourists still come by the planeload to stay in the all-inclusive resorts found in Montego Bay, Negril, and Ocho Rios. Cruise ships sail into the harbors of

Jamaica, and for a few hours thousands of vacationers board buses to see as much as they can in the few hours allotted to them. After this quick look, they return to their ships and sail to the next port of call. It's a nice way to travel, but all-inclusive resorts and cruise ships don't give you any real understanding of a country and its people.

Many affluent Americans say they don't like to visit countries like Jamaica because of the extreme poverty they see many people experiencing. It's the kind of thinking that says this: If I can't see your pain, then I don't have to deal with it. I may know in my mind that you are hurting, but if I don't look into your hungry eyes or feel the touch of your outstretched hand then I can play without guilt.

Certainly we cannot take on all the problems of our world, but we also cannot pretend they are not there. Around our globe, millions of people are struggling to feed themselves and their families. And those of us who are blessed with more must not turn our backs on our brothers and sisters. What happens to anyone indirectly affects everyone.

I wish that every young person in America could spend some time living in a so-called third world country. I think it would help the person understand that many of the things we take for granted are considered by much of the world to be luxuries beyond reach.

One of the best ideas to come out of the '60s was the Peace Corps, because it not only assists people in the countries where the volunteers serve, it helps the volunteers even more. When you live and work with people, you realize how much alike we all are and how much there is for us to learn from one another.

For instance, I thought I came here to write, but I realize now that I am here to learn. We all have heard that life is a school, and it must be. Every person, every experience is a part of our curriculum; if we view our life experience with our inner vision, we can see the meaning—the purpose of each assignment.

In times of crisis and despair, we cry out, "Why, why is this happening to me?" We lament, "If there is a God, why does He, or She, allow human beings to suffer so—why?" I don't believe it is God who allows suffering; it is we who allow it. Each one of us is a living expression of life, and how we live that life is our choice. We human beings seem to be such slow learners; we repeat the same mistakes over and over. Look at our history: wars to end wars, religious wars, and ethnic wars. And with each new war, we develop more lethal, sophisticated ways to kill one another. Does God do this? Of course not, we do it.

Why do we do it? We do it because we have not learned the most important lesson life has to teach us. For some reason, we refuse to practice the basic law of life that has been expounded by all the great teachers of the world—Jesus' first commandment. Remember when the scribe asked him in Mark 12:28, "Which commandment is the first of all?"

He answered: "The first is, 'Hear, O Israel: the Lord our God, the Lord is one; you shall love the Lord your God with all your heart, and with all your soul, and with all your mind, and with all your strength.' The second is this: 'You shall love your neighbor as yourself.' There is no other commandment greater than these" (Mk. 12:29-31).

But for some reason we refuse to heed his admonition, and we continue to try to solve our problems in painful and destructive ways. I wonder why it is so difficult for us to love one another and ourselves, when it is love that we all are seeking.

Yesterday I was watching Devon as he moved quickly from task to task. And I asked, "Devon, why is it that some days you are filled with such amazing energy and on other days you hardly move at all?"

Devon's quick reply was "that's just how my spirit travels." I looked closely at this young man who was so comfortable with himself and his surroundings. Whether he was paddling his canoe or climbing a tree to pick a coconut to share with us, his movements were naturally graceful and sure. All my life I have been around people who lectured, wrote, and preached about how to feel and experience God in our lives. In this young Jamaican man, I felt a serenity of spirit that I am sure was not searched for or found through reading "how-to" books or listening to intellectual dissertations. Rather it was simply there—like his arms and legs. I believe that it is simply there in every one of us too, but

Top: Devon Myers, Rosemary's Jamaican guide.
Bottom: Lorna Cheong, Rosemary, and Devon.

we have lost our awareness of its presence, since our world has gotten more and more complex.

Soon we will be leaving Jamaica. My friend is eager to go. I doubt he will return to this island. What I found soothing he found boring. I will always be grateful to him for finding Sea Star, and I'm only sorry that it didn't do for him what it has done for me. I will come back to Jamaica. It has caught me in its enchanted web, and I know this island has much to teach me. They say here that "nothing happens before its time," and so for now I will honor my spirit's travel, and when it is time I will return.

## Soft Winds—1998

I'm back in Jamaica. It happened more quickly than I had thought possible. But when something is supposed to be, ways open that we have not imagined.

This time I'm living in a different part of the island—Montego Bay. My house sits on a hill and looks to the sea. It is called Soft Winds, and as Sea Star was, this one, too, is aptly named. Bougainvillea bushes circle a lovely garden, and their blossoms dance continuously to the music of the winds that blow softly from the sea.

I chose Montego Bay because I am impressed by the work a Jamaican friend, Pearl Davis, is doing here. Twenty years ago she became the minister of the Unity Faith Center. And, along with her church ministry, she has established an outstanding kindergarten and preparatory school.

Countries like Jamaica that have a history of slavery and hundreds of years of exploitation and colonization are left with a feeling of inferiority and victimization. To change these feelings, Jamaicans must cultivate a new vision of themselves and their relationship to the world. This is what Pearl is endeavoring to develop in the children she teaches. Along with their regular class work, she is helping them understand that they have within them all the attributes they need to make their lives successful and productive. She is teaching them not only to love themselves but also to nourish and express their individual gifts.

Pearl's school has an enrollment of some 400 students. In Jamaica, because there are a limited number of high schools, children must take a difficult exam before they are accepted into a secondary school. Seventy-five percent of Pearl's students pass the exam, and not only do they finish high school but many go on to college. It is my belief that the spiritual principles these children are learning along with their intellectual education will have a profound effect on the future of Jamaica.

Last night I was having dinner with friends when they began discussing some of the many challenges facing their beautiful island. Kingston, the largest city and the capital, has the dubious distinction of being one of the world's most violent cities. The inner city of Kingston is the home of many of Jamaica's poorest people. It is overcrowded, and living conditions are extremely bad. It is a place of despair and hopelessness, a fertile breeding ground for crime and violence and, if conditions are not improved, for possible anarchy.

My friends are concerned because the frustration and unrest in Kingston are spreading throughout the island. It is like a river of discontent whose rising waters can no longer be contained within its banks. The three-fold challenge of Jamaica—over-population, poverty, and pollution—is a microcosm of what our whole world must solve if we are to bring forth a "new heaven and a new earth" in the twenty-first century.

I have faith that Jamaica's people will move through these turbulent times with their usual resilience and resourcefulness. There is a joke Jamaicans tell that says, "If you are sent to hell, be sure you take a Jamaican with you, because they can always find a way out!"

One of my young dinner guests concluded our evening conversation by saying, "I dream of a time when Jamaica will be a place where there is no hunger, no crime, no fear." He said, "I guess I'm visualizing a kind of spiritual community where people come together in peace and harmony to pursue a common vision."

As I listened to his words, I knew the kind of community he was visualizing. This young man had just described the place where I was born.

Rosemary—the only person born at Unity Farm.

# 1. Unity Farm

Once upon a time there was a place, an almost mythological place, situated in the very heart of America. It was there that I was born, and it was there that I spent my childhood. When I was growing up I had no idea how fortunate I was to live in such a place or what a remarkable family I was blessed to be a part of.

Unity Farm, as it was called at the time of my birth, was inhabited by a group of wonderful, imaginative souls who had a collective vision. In retrospect, I call it their magnificent obsession. They dreamed of building a city of God where people of all races, all cultures, and all religions could experience their oneness in God.

The idea began with my grandparents, Charles and Myrtle Fillmore. One spring night, well over a hundred years ago, my grandmother, a frail, sick woman, walked into a lecture hall in Kansas City, Missouri, and came away with an idea that was to change her life. This idea was not to let go of her until she and my grandfather—who was soon set afire with it too—had founded a faith that eventually reached around the globe and blessed the lives of millions of people throughout the twentieth century and now beyond.

In one hour, her whole outlook toward herself and her world changed. The simple, divine idea that she was the beloved child of God, that God's will for her could only be perfect life and wholeness, filled her mind and flowed through her body.

The old belief that she was an invalid, that she had been born frail and weak, that her time on Earth was limited, was washed away. Over and over she repeated to herself: *I am a child of God, and therefore I do not inherit sickness. I am a child of God, and therefore I do not inherit sickness.* In two years my grandmother was healed of the tuberculosis that was supposed to have taken her life. People learned of her healing and came to her for help, and they, too, found healing.

My grandfather had also been in physical pain most of his life due to a childhood skating accident that had left one of his legs withered and much shorter than the other. He saw what was happening to people who came to pray with his wife, but he had an inquiring, scientific mind and could not accept things on blind faith. He began searching for an answer to the amazing healings that were taking place in their living room. First, he read all the books he could find on religion and science. But the more he read, the more confused he became, as there were so many conflicting theories and theologies. So he finally decided if he was to find the Truth, he had to, as he described it, "go directly to headquarters—to God."

Night after night he would sit in silence, waiting for

God to speak to him. He affirmed words of Truth, of life, and finally he made his breakthrough and his healing began. He wrote: "My chronic pains ceased. My hip healed and grew stronger, and my leg lengthened until in a few years I dispensed with the steel extension that I had worn since I was a child."[1] So Charles joined with Myrtle and together they founded a school of what they called "Practical Christianity," and they named it Unity. They became magnificently obsessed with the idea that if they committed themselves to the Spirit of God within them, God would do the rest. They had absolute faith that if they put God first, they would be healed, they would be prospered, they would be free.

They dreamed of a healing center that would reach around the world to inspire all people to move beyond their humanness into a conscious awareness of who they really are. This dream became a reality for them because they truly believed that "with God all things are possible." They had proved this with their own healing. Two sick, poverty-stricken people found a faith. They made the quantum leap from darkness and despair into the light of all possibilities.

Many books have been written about my grandparents and the growth of the Unity movement, how they began a center in Kansas City and eventually moved to the country to found a spiritual city that is also an incorporated town. I will not try to cover what others have researched and written about so extensively. Instead, I will share what it was like for me to grow up in such unique surroundings and with such committed, loving people.

Until I was twelve years old, I had a childhood as nearly perfect as anyone could possibly have. Unity Farm was an idyllic place for a child. It provided all those things that children enjoy. In my growing-up years, it was not only a spiritual community, it was also a working farm—there were orchards, vineyards, and crops in cultivation. There were chickens, cows, horses, ponies, and dogs. Since it allowed no hunting, Unity Farm also teemed with wildlife: deer, foxes, coyotes, rabbits, squirrels, chipmunks, and many kinds of birds.

Recreational facilities for the people who worked for Unity included a swimming pool, golf course, tennis courts, clubhouse for parties, playground, picnic grounds, vacation cottages, and a beautiful amphitheater for summer theater and concerts. There were lakes and ponds for boating and fishing, and there were woods to roam. Each season brought with it special activities and celebrations.

Francis Gable wrote a wonderful poem during the 1920s that captured the spirit of the place.

### Unity Farm
Nestling over hill and dale;
Giant rocks and lowly swale;
While the sturdy hardwood trees
Rustle 'neath each balmy breeze;
Like a velvet carpet green,

Rolling visitors may be seen,
Touched by shade spots, dark and cool,
All surrounding limpit pool;

Beauty framed by nature's plan,
Other joy nooks shaped by man;
Fairest spot to which to roam,
This is Unity's new home.[2]

In the spring, the fragrance of thousands of apple blossoms heralded the coming of May. The advent of spring was celebrated with the crowning of a May queen, maypole dances, and the mysterious arrival of May baskets filled with spring flowers, found outside your doors in the early morn.

Summer was perhaps the best time of all. Lazy days in the swimming pool, tennis and golf for those who wanted to exercise that much. Saturday night dances under the stars. Sunday night band concerts, even a soda fountain for any kind of ice cream concoction you might desire.

In the fall there were long walks through the woods, marshmallow and wiener roasts at the picnic grounds, drives through the orchards to see trees laden with ripe red and golden apples ready to be picked and sold at the fruit stand that was on the highway running by the farm. People came by the carloads from all the surrounding communities to take home baskets of apples, fresh pure cider, and plump sweet grapes.

Winter was a time for ice-skating, sledding, warm crackling fires, and of course Christmas—the grandest celebration of all. There were Christmas programs, candlelighting services, and the magic of Christmas morning when my brother and I awakened at the crack of dawn to discover what Santa had left us. My childhood was filled with so much love and joy that it is difficult for me to describe for you the beauty and wonder of that place called Unity Farm.

The people who lived and cared for Unity Farm could have stepped out of any of the books of fairy tales that my grandmother brought us to read. There was Uncle George, an elderly gentleman who tended the vegetable gardens with a vengeance. This was his territory, and no one was to pick anything without his approval. I have no idea why we called him Uncle George, as he was not our uncle or anyone else's I knew of. My grandfather loved to tell the story of how Uncle George chased him out of his garden with a pitchfork because he picked cucumbers without asking his permission. Uncle George loved his vegetables, and they grew bountifully under his care. He didn't have much use for human communication; but when it came to tomatoes, carrots, onions, and cucumbers, his rapport was without equal.

And then there was Miss Bea Narrimore. She kept the hotel, which was actually a large English Tudor house overlooking the swimming pool and golf course. Miss Narrimore was a southern lady from New Orleans who looked as though she had wandered away from a Tennessee Williams play or a Faulkner novel. She had a wistful, fragile beauty that was enhanced by her soft dresses and her quiet southern speech. I always suspected that she was the one who left the May baskets outside our door because there was a whimsical quality about her that enjoyed surprises.

I have no idea how she got to Unity Farm or what her history was. I only know that she was there throughout my childhood—a gentle reminder always of grace and beauty and southern hospitality. If you stopped by to see her, there were always crumpets and tea or lemonade and cookies. And if you walked by on a warm summer evening, you could hear the music of Chopin or Mozart drifting through her open window. She was an accomplished pianist, but she played mostly in the evening when she was alone. I often wondered what memories were released as her fingers danced in the night.

Junie, who kept the clubhouse and swimming pool, was as opposite from Miss Narrimore as night is from day. Where Miss Bea was ethereal, Junie was as down to earth as an apple pie. Like Uncle George with his garden, she ruled her domain with an iron hand. However, her bark was much worse than her bite. In summer she sat in the little house by the pool and signed people in and out. She made sure that lifeguards were diligent and that there was no roughhousing around the pool. She put Band-Aids on skinned knees and soothed bruised feelings. She was the lady in charge. In the winter, her role changed; she then became the hostess of the clubhouse. I can recall many nights I spent by the fire with Junie and my dear Helen—my friend and my nanny—playing games, eating popcorn, roasting marshmallows. Sometimes we were joined by Mr. Lucky. Lucky lived in the Unity Tower which was then, and is now, the landmark of Unity. He was a gentle soul, an accountant by profession, who said little but was always ready to help with what needed to be done. Mr. Lucky was my friend, and I always especially enjoyed the evenings he came to play a game of Monopoly or Hearts with us.

The day my mother died my family sent Lucky to pick me up at school. I was relieved that it was him they sent, because I knew that I wouldn't have to talk and neither would he. But there would be comfort in his presence.

When Mr. Lucky passed away, after I had grown up, I cried more at his funeral than I have cried at any other person's death. I think it was not only that I had lost a dear friend, but he also represented to me all those lovely people who were a part of my childhood and a part of the magic that permeated every nook and corner of that place called Unity Farm. Each person who lived and worked there brought a quality that was integral to the grand design.

Even many of their names were picturesque. For instance, there were Mr. and Mrs. Corn. Mr. Corn cared for the orchards, and under his loving supervision the trees responded by providing the best apples in the county. When Mr. Corn left, the orchards seemed to lose their enthusiasm. The friend who had so loved and encouraged them was gone, and those who followed could not take his place. His wife, Mrs. Corn, was an accomplished musician who played the organ for the church. Mrs. Bergen, whose husband also worked on the farm, joined with Mrs. Corn to play not only for services but also for Saturday night dances at the clubhouse. And then there were Mr. and Mrs. Pig, May, Eve, and Aunt Pharaby, not related to Uncle George. Aunt Pharaby was the librarian. She always kept a jar of candy on her desk, which she shared with anyone who checked out a book. There were, of course, families who lived and worked on the farm who had more prosaic names but were equally important in the creation of Unity Farm.

In the movie *A Field of Dreams* there is a line that says, "If you build it they will come." When the Fillmore's envisioned a city of God "they came to *build* it"—farmers, carpenters, stonemasons, wood-carvers gathered together to build a spiritual city, a New Jerusalem. If you walk around Unity Village today, you feel the spirit of these people as you view lovely rock walls bordering green slopes of grass, gardens surrounded by lilac bushes, flowing fountains encircled by gardens of roses, beautiful hand-carved doors opening into tranquil reception halls, graceful archways filled with decorative wrought iron flower receptacles. Everywhere you see beauty. The artistry expressed in the intricate details of the work of these craftsmen is most unusual and must have been inspired by the same spiritual energy that drew these amazing people to Unity.

Myrtle Page Fillmore and Charles S. Fillmore.

# 2. The Family

When I was very young, there were four generations of Fillmores living at Unity Farm. My great-grandmother lived in the white farmhouse that was part of the original parcel of land bought by my family. Right across the road from her home my father built a residence for my grandparents. He called it "The Arches" because graceful arches enclosed the terrace, which looked out to the Unity Tower. Since the offices of Unity were in Kansas City, my grandparents came to the farm mostly on weekends. Because my grandmother did not enjoy cooking, the home had no kitchen, and Myrtle and Charles ate their meals at Grandmother Fillmore's when they were there.

Our home was within easy walking distance of Grandmother Fillmore's. The first and second holes of the golf course were built between our two homes. And then there was the house of my Uncle Lowell and Aunt Alice, which was built above the swimming pool area. It was the largest and most imposing of our four family homes and the last one to be constructed. The Fillmores were a close-knit family, and each one of their homes was filled with many happy memories of meals shared, holiday celebrations, and childhood play.

Although other people now are living in all our family homes, in my dreams I'm always back at Unity Farm in the house where I was born. It contains so much of my history: both of my parents died there, I was married there and so were both of my children. My soul is deeply connected to that home, and no matter where I travel, my subconscious keeps taking me back to my parents' house.

Each member of the Fillmore family played a vital role in the development of Unity. It was as if a group of souls, in that unknown place from whence we all come, were designated to come to Earth to bring forth a new concept of living. Their mission began with Myrtle's healing, followed by Charles' revelation, and then the ability of their three sons to bring the spiritual into material manifestation.

Lowell, the oldest son, was deeply committed to the principles his parents espoused, and he spent his entire life helping disseminate Unity's healing message. Rick Fillmore, my father, was the architect whose dream of building an American utopia materialized as Unity Farm, which then became Unity Village. Although Royal, the youngest son, died when he was thirty-seven years old, he, too, made an important contribution to Unity's growth. He was very active in community affairs and worked closely with his mother in the development of *Wee Wisdom* magazine.

One thing I know for sure is that Myrtle Fillmore's three sons loved and respected their mother. My memories of my grandmother are dim, for I was only six when she died. But my father spoke so glowingly of his mother that I feel I have some knowledge of what a remarkable woman she was.

In my mind's eye, I remember she had a crown of white hair and wore lovely flowing pastel gowns. I have many books she brought us: mine were fairy tales and classic children's stories. My dad always said that his mother lived in a place that few of us know; she was an ethereal being who was more at home in the realm of spirit than in the world.

However, she did amazing things for a woman of her time in history. She was born in 1845, almost two decades before the Civil War. Her parents were Ohio farmers, Marcus and Lucy Page. The eighth of nine children, Myrtle was raised as a strict Methodist. Her given name was Mary Caroline, but she never liked it and decided she wanted to be called Myrtle instead. After high school, she wrote for a newspaper in Columbus, Ohio. When she was twenty-one years old, she enrolled in Oberlin College and took the literary course for ladies. This only lasted for a year, because women at that time could not take a full four-year course. She then accepted a teaching position in Clinton, Missouri, and there began her life interest in children.

Far ahead of her time, Myrtle refused to let conventional thinking keep her from moving forward on her spiritual journey. Her fragile health took her to Denison, Texas, where, hopefully, a warmer climate would help her lungs. There she met and fell in love with my grandfather, who was nine years younger than she. He was a young man eager to make his fortune in the mining towns of the West. So this frail 35-year-old schoolmarm from a sheltered, Methodist upbringing joined her young husband to travel in stagecoaches over treacherous mountain passes to the boomtowns of Colorado; first Gunnison, then to Pueblo where their first two sons were born. From Colorado, they went to Omaha, Nebraska, and finally to Kansas City in 1885, where they stayed.

If you believe in destiny, surely Charles and Myrtle were destined to come together. Theirs was a love that not only enriched their lives in amazing ways but enriched the lives of millions of others throughout the twentieth century and continues to do so as we travel the twenty-first century.

In my very early years, my great-grandmother's home was the family meeting place. She was the matriarch and dearly loved by her grandsons and by her son Charles. Charles and his mother had made a long journey together—one that took them from an Indian reservation in North Minnesota to frontier towns in Colorado and Texas and finally to Kansas City, Missouri. She was a small lady, who in her later years looked like a dowager Queen Mother. Seeing her, it was difficult to believe what a long and arduous journey she had survived.

She had migrated to the United States from Nova Scotia. At a very young age she married a hunter and trapper who left her to raise two boys by herself in the northern wilderness. Her son Norton also went away as soon as he was old enough. Charles, left alone with his mother, formed a strong bond that was to last throughout her lifetime. And a long life she had! She was 99 years old when she died, but her son and grandsons made sure that her last years were much more comfortable than her difficult early ones.

My grandmother, Mama Myrtle as we called her, was ill much of the time when her sons were young. Grandmother Fillmore was there to care for the three boys and to do the cooking and household chores. I have often wondered how Myrtle felt about having her mother-in-law as part of her household almost from the very beginning of her marriage. I'm sure it helped her in many ways, especially after she and Charles began the Unity work. These women were like Martha and Mary in the New Testament. Great-grandmother took care of the material needs of the family: food, clothing, and those things needed to sustain everyday life. Mama Myrtle provided the spiritual sustenance. Since she had been a schoolteacher before she married Charles, she had great interest in not only teaching her sons spiritual principles but also instilling in them the importance of discipline and study. Myrtle loved children, and one of the most important contributions she made to the Unity work was the creation of a magazine for youngsters called *Wee Wisdom*, which was published for 100 years.

My immediate family was quite small: my mother, father, and my brother Charles. Charles is four years older than I. He and my cousin Frances, Royal Fillmore's daughter, are the same age. Both of Frances's parents died when she was very young, her mother right after she was born and her father when she was just two years old. She was raised by Uncle Lowell and Aunt Alice, who had no children of their own. But Fran, as we called her, was like a sister to Charles and me and was very much a part of our family. In childhood and adolescence, four or five years can make a big difference; since Charles and Fran were the same age, they had many common interests that didn't always include a baby sister. Perhaps that is why I spent so much time with my father and grandfather.

The two people who had the most influence on my early life were without a doubt these men. They formed my perception of what the male species is like, and I think unconsciously I have always looked for their qualities in all the men I have met along the way.

My father and grandfather were great friends, alike in many ways and yet very different also. When I knew my grandfather, Papa Charlie as we called him, he was in his older years. He was a small, slender man with an elfin face, which shone with the sparkle of a young boy about to embark on some exciting adventure. He wore graceful bow ties and always smelled of sweet cologne. As far back as I can remember he would come to our home for Saturday night dinners. I would run down the back stone steps of the house to greet him. It was always such a joy for me to be in his presence. I liked to sit close to him and hold his hand. I realize now it was because there was a magnetic aura around him that drew you into his light. I never thought of him as a mystic or guru; he was my grandfather, and if I had searched the world, I could not have found a better one. He liked to do all the things kids like: he enjoyed picnics, movies, ice cream, jokes, and exploring new places. His childhood accident left him with a limp, but that didn't dampen his enthusiasm for going places or doing things. Although he never actually drove a car, he was one of the original backseat drivers—a quality I unfortunately inherited.

I remember one time our whole family piled into the car and went to the Missouri Ozarks. My grandfather always sat in front next to my father, who would drive. If a road looked untraveled and led off into the wilderness, Papa Charlie would always say, "Let's try this road, Rick." My father would reluctantly do it, and perhaps we would go for miles and find a dead end—but we would also see interesting, new things that we would have missed had we stayed on the paved, well-traveled highway. The unknown was always exciting to Charles Fillmore. He had the spirit of a true adventurer, and he was constantly exploring new dimensions of living and thinking.

In his later years he discovered California and fell in love with it. He and his second wife Cora bought a house in Sherman Oaks and spent their winters there. At that time I was attending school at the Pasadena Playhouse, and I would go to visit them on weekends. He loved California not only for its beauty and weather but most important for its openness to new paradigms.

When I reflect on how fearlessly he lived his life, I'm always in awe of his courage and resilience. When I was young, I wasn't cognizant of how different he was from most of us. I was not a very perceptive kid; like most young people, my world revolved pretty much around myself. Having lived my life at Unity Farm, I had a very limited knowledge of the outside world. However, when I started school in the little town of Lee's Summit, Missouri, I discovered there was a vast difference between my family and the families of my school friends. For instance, I learned very quickly that there were no vegetarians in my school, that no other kid had a grandfather who sat in the "silence," and that most people called the doctor when they got sick instead of their grandfather.

These facts were very surprising to me, particularly that there were no vegetarians, because all my relatives were vegetarians—except my father and mother. Unity had a cafeteria that served neither meat nor fish. I never questioned this as strange. We had meat at our home, but when we went to my Uncle Lowell's home, we ate vegetables; when my grandfather came to our house, Helen, our wonderful housekeeper, always prepared him special meat-free dishes. In my child's mind, I just figured that it was everyone's choice to eat what he or she wanted. I had never felt any pressure to become a vegetarian. In fact, my grandfather knew how much I liked fried chicken; so when he performed a wedding that was followed by a wedding party at a local farm that was serving a chicken dinner, he would call and tell me to meet him outside the Unity Chapel at such and such a time. I would eagerly wait for the wedding to be over so I could jump in the car beside him, and together we would go to the party. I don't think he ever explained my presence, so I'm sure many puzzled brides and grooms wondered who the funny little girl was who came to eat the minister's chicken.

When my school friends would invite me to their homes for dinner, much to my dismay, I would find that their mothers had gone to much trouble to fix special vegetarian dinners for me. They thought anyone connected to Unity must not eat meat. I suffered through those dinners with as much politeness as I could muster, but I found it challenging for I really didn't like most vegetables. Someone took a picture of my brother and cousin once, and it was published in some health magazine with the caption: "The boy eats meat and the girl doesn't." I used to study the picture to see if there was any difference between the two—but couldn't find it. They both looked equally healthy and well-fed.

Looking back, I am tremendously appreciative of the people in Lee's Summit. Their acceptance of Unity and its different kind of thinking was truly amazing. This was a small southern town in the 1930s and 1940s, long before meditation and vegetarianism were popular, long before New Age gurus were on the best-seller lists and *Larry King Live*. It was a town of 1300 people who were mostly Baptists, Methodists, and Presbyterians, with a small number of Catholics and Episcopalians, and to my knowledge only one Jewish family. If the citizens of Lee's Summit were suspicious of this unusual religious group that had moved into their rural community—and I'm sure they were—they hid it well. We were warmly welcomed into their schools, their homes, and their places of business. I have many wonderful memories of my school years there. Lee's Summit is no longer a small town; with a population of 70,000 and counting, it is now the fastest growing community in the state of Missouri. However, when I graduated from high school there were only thirty-five in our class, and of course I knew every one of them. Today I still have wonderful friends who were former classmates. In fact, one of my best friends, Billie Bell, I first met when we were in kindergarten together. Billie grew up to be Dr. William Bell, a wonderful doctor who served the people of Lee's Summit tirelessly until his recent retirement.

After I started school, I began inviting my schoolmates to visit. My grandfather, when he was not involved in conversation or writing, would meditate—what he called going into the "silence." It was so much a part of him, so natural, I thought everyone's grandfather probably did the same thing. But I soon discovered this was not true. When my young friends came, they would say: "What's wrong with your grandfather? Why is he sitting there with his eyes closed? Is he asleep? Why does his body jump once in a while?" I couldn't understand why they thought this was strange. I would just tell them that he was in the "silence." Didn't their grandfathers go into the "silence," for heaven's sake? No, their grandfathers didn't go into any silence, and they had never heard of it before, and what in the world was I talking about anyway? I would try to explain that it was sort of like praying, and the reason he jerked once in a while was because he would be touched by the energy of Spirit. The kids would look at me like either I, my grandfather, or possibly both of us were crazy and hurriedly suggest that we should go outside and play. I have no idea how they relayed this to their parents. Maybe they were smart enough not to discuss it at home, since they liked to come to the Farm where there were so many places to explore and so many things to do.

I also discovered from my classmates that most people call doctors, not spiritual healers, when they are sick. Once after some childhood illness, I returned to school, and someone asked if I had had to have the doctor come to our home (this was when doctors actually made house calls). I replied: "Oh, no, we never call a doctor. We call my grandfather and he comes."

"Your grandfather? What can he do?"

I thought, Oh, no, here we go again!

"Well," I would tell them, "my grandfather comes and sits by my bed and goes into the 'silence.'"

"What?"

"The 'silence.' He prays for me. Then I go to sleep, and I get well. What's so weird about that?" Once again I realized my grandfather was not just a run-of-the-mill person—he was different.

When I was in school in California, one weekend I was visiting friends and dislocated my knee. It looked awful; the kneecap slipped and the front went to the back with the bone sticking straight out. I was in a great deal of pain, plus each time I looked at my knee I was scared out of my wits. The mother of my friends frantically called my grandfather who fortunately was in Sherman Oaks at the time. He told her not to worry, that it would be just fine; all she had to do was give it a quick jerk, and it would go right back in place. The woman was too frightened to attempt that and, instead, called a chiropractor who knew someone who treated wrestlers. He came and did exactly what my grandfather had suggested, gave my leg a quick jerk, and my knee slid back into place. I don't know how my grandfather, sitting across town, knew exactly what to do, for I had never had this happen to me before, but he knew. My friend's mother, after getting over the trauma of having to deal with me and my knee, was impressed that my grandfather was so calm and assured while she and I were in a state of panic.

With my long history in Unity, I have known a great

many people who were involved in the world of religion: ministers, writers, teachers, self-proclaimed gurus of every kind. But never have I met anyone who was like my grandfather. He was unpretentious; his ego was never on display. Wherever he was, whomever he was with, he was always exactly the same. If he was unhappy or angry at times, I never saw it.

I had a friend who used to say about some minister, "He is so spiritual that he is no earthly good." And I could certainly relate to that statement because many people get so into their religiosity that you seek to avoid their "holy superiority" if you want to have fun. But this was certainly not true of my grandfather. He loved life, every aspect of it. Even when he was in his late eighties and early nineties, he was ready to go to the movies, shopping, or whatever. He especially enjoyed movies, westerns in particular. It was no problem to get him to take us to the little theatre in Lee's Summit, and at that time the show changed every two or three days.

When I became a teenager and had dates on Saturdays, he would always inquire if we were going to the movies. Most of the time we were, but no matter how much I loved him I wasn't about to take him with me on a date. Now I wish I would have had the courage to say to my date, "Hey, you don't mind if my grandfather tags along—he'll even pay our way and take us for a soda afterwards." Can you imagine the look on my date's face? He'd probably say, "Well, I don't know—how old is your grandfather?" "Oh, he's about ninety or so—but he's lots of fun." I wish I had done that, because he *was* fun and certainly more entertaining than most of my dates.

My grandfather also liked to listen to music on the radio, and he especially liked the "Hit Parade," a program that was on every Saturday night. His favorite singer on the program was Wee Bonnie Baker, and he loved it when she sang "Oh, Johnny, How You Can Love." At that time I liked to imagine that someday I would be a famous dancer, so I would dance to every song they played, and my grandfather would reward me with enthusiastic applause. My father wasn't that impressed and suggested that perhaps I should find another profession, but with my grandfather's encouragement, I refused to be discouraged about my talent. After a while and a few dance lessons, I decided perhaps my father was right and I would instead be a famous movie actress. My grandfather thought that was a good idea too. He had a way of making you feel good about yourself. He firmly believed that you could do whatever you wanted to do. When I was attending school at the Pasadena Playhouse, he called me and said that Spirit had told him that someday I would be in the movies. Well, at that time I could not imagine myself in films. Although I had wanted to be an actress, now my focus was on radio. I had come to the realization during my tenure at the Playhouse that my talent as an actress was not outstanding, and my physical appearance did not herald a great career in the motion picture industry. I started to explain all of this to him. But he said, "No, Spirit doesn't make mistakes." When I speak of Spirit revealing things to him, I mean it was his way of saying that in meditation, in the silence, an inner voice gave him instruction and guidance. Well, Spirit and Papa Charlie were right, if not in the way I envisioned!

When he told me this, television had not become a part of our culture, but when it did, I moved from radio into television broadcasting and worked both before and behind the camera for thirty years. In the beginning I was a spokesperson for Unity with a five-minute program built around *Daily Word* magazine, and later I became coproducer of the *Word From Unity*. Papa Charlie had passed on before I went into television, but if he had been here, he would have been thrilled. When radio came into being, Unity had one of the first religious broadcasting stations in the United States, and my grandfather had a nightly program. He was always searching for new ways to introduce the message of Unity to the world. He would have embraced television with great enthusiasm.

My grandfather had little formal education, but he was an avid reader and could recite Shakespeare verbatim. On those Saturday nights at our house, he and my father would talk late into the night, discussing everything from their visions for a Unity City to the newest scientific breakthroughs in technology, physics, or whatever. They lived in a world of ideas, and Papa Charlie's mind was always pushing him forward into new frontiers of spiritual thought. People would sometimes point out to him that he would contradict in a lecture something he had previously written about. This did not faze him. He would reply, "If I said it then, I meant it then—but Spirit has revealed that I was wrong in that assumption."

What other people thought about him made little difference to him. The substance of Charles' and Myrtle's teaching was based on Jesus Christ's teachings. They found that the words of Jesus could be literally applied to daily living and bring miraculous results. Hence the name "Practical Christianity." It was never the Fillmores' intention to start a new religion. They simply wanted to share what they were learning with others. This seemed like a very simple and natural understanding of The Gospels to them, yet Charles Fillmore was sometimes called "sacrilegious," just because he insisted on taking Jesus' words literally, statements such as: "The one who believes in me will also do the works that I do and, in fact, will do greater works than these" (Jn. 14:12).

People love to read Jesus' teachings, but we tend to back off some when it comes to living them. We are liable to say of some teachings: "That's fine and wonderful, but in today's world they are just not practical." Maybe it isn't practical to turn the other cheek, go the second mile, and love your enemies. At least it isn't practical unless you are really willing to trust God. But Charles Fillmore didn't care if some ideas seemed practical or not. When he believed, he believed all the way. He refused to compromise with negation.

Once my father told me this story: Unity had a lawyer who was always looking at things the way lawyers are taught to do. It was during the depression when times certainly didn't look good, and this lawyer was in a meeting where Unity's future was being discussed. The lawyer pointed out everything that was wrong with Unity. The future, as far as he was concerned, was not bright; if things continued the way they were going, Unity would surely go down the proverbial drain. They were in the red, and they couldn't stay afloat if things weren't run in a more businesslike way. As far as he was concerned, he was dealing with a group of crazy idealists who put dreams ahead of good sense.

My grandfather listened to this man for quite a while and then quietly asked him to leave. He explained to him that he couldn't have someone working for Unity who felt as he did. He said Unity is not a business—it is God's work—and his kind of thinking could only limit Unity. This is not to say that Charles was not practical; he was very practical. Before Unity, he had been very successful in the real estate business. In fact, several streets in Kansas City were named by him. He knew you must put legs to your dreams, but he also knew the power of thought and that if you surround yourself with naysayers, you are creating unnecessary barriers which keep your good from you.[3]

When I look at Unity Village, I see, without equivocation, a place that was built on faith. There were times in the early years when people had to wait for their paychecks, but they wouldn't leave; and in the end everyone was compensated. Someone asked my grandmother once, "What will we do if the money runs out?"

She quickly replied, "It's not the money you should be concerned about—we must pray that our faith doesn't run out."

And of course it never did. Before the buildings were actually built, my father created a miniature concept of the future Unity City so people could see how it would look. Today it is exactly as he planned it. He also landscaped the grounds where the buildings eventually would be built. And not one member of the family doubted for a moment that the buildings would be built, that Unity Farm would become Unity Village, and that eventually Unity City would come into manifestation.

I remember reading in one of the old issues of *Unity Magazine* an article in which my grandfather said some people had been taking him to task for writing about regeneration of the physical body. They had apparently been telling him he shouldn't write about living forever in this body because, after all, he was getting on in years, and if he should pass on after declaring these beliefs, it would be a blow to the Truth he taught. He just laughed and said he was going to keep right on believing in regeneration and writing about it whenever he wanted to. And he said, "Like Napoleon's drummer boy, I cannot beat retreat." I can just hear him saying that. He marched under a banner that said, "No compromise with the world of negation." He didn't know how to hedge. He once wrote that it was disobedience to Spirit to "refuse to do right at all hazards."

I think my grandfather's complete confidence in God has a tendency to scare us just a little, but I think it was the secret of his life. Every great person has been this kind of "no compromise" thinker. The world has often condemned such people as self-willed, foolish, and impractical—but these are the people who have moved the world because they themselves could not be moved by it.

Now, some hundred years later, science is discovering that Charles Fillmore was right—that our body renews itself continuously. Every seven years we have a completely new body, and some scientists now feel that perhaps we get old because at some time we decide that aging is inevitable. Or, as Charles Fillmore stated, "We get old because we think old thoughts." The new science of quantum physics is confirming many of Unity's teachings. My grandfather thought that Unity would be the spiritual catalyst which could help bridge the gulf which has separated science and religion. And that when science and religion finally do come together, miracles will happen which are beyond our present comprehension. He felt that the splitting of the atom would change our world forever and of course it has.

Whenever I get discouraged or depressed, I think of my grandfather and his indomitable spirit. He began his life in the northern wilderness on an Indian reservation on the South River, near St. Cloud, Minnesota. His father was a fur trader with the Chippewa Indians. When he was ten years old, as I mentioned earlier, he had a bad skating accident that left him with tuberculosis of the hip, which the doctor predicted would kill him before he reached forty. Besides being in almost constant pain, he had one leg that was several inches shorter than the other. It was necessary for him to walk with braces, a built-up shoe, and crutches. However, he still had the fortitude when he was just nineteen to leave Minnesota and seek his fortune in the boomtowns of the West. First to Caddo, Oklahoma, which at that time (1874) was Indian territory and considered to be one of the wildest towns in the West. It must have been too wild for him because soon he moved to Dennison, Texas, where he met the woman who was to change his life.

Charles Fillmore's journey was remarkable: he overcame so many obstacles. Nothing could stop him—pain, a lack of education, poverty. His restless spirit kept him moving, searching, until he found a faith that brought peace to his restless soul, freed his body of pain, and gave him a mission, which he passionately pursued as long as he remained on Earth.

Was it just by chance that both he and Myrtle came together in Texas? Was it just by chance that both of them were healed of physical challenges that normally would have been fatal? Was it by chance that together they founded a faith that reaches around the world? Was it by chance that each of their sons had a special talent that was vitally important to the growth and enfoldment of Unity? Well, that's a lot of chance. Perhaps a great deal of what we call chance is in truth a divine plan that is active in the life of each one of us.

Marcus Bach, in his book *The World of Serendipity*, writes: "To see ourselves as a part of a universal plan … to realize that there are dimensions beyond the commonly seen and experiences beyond the ordinarily felt, these are enriching qualities. Everything about life points to the fact that we are not alone, that our faith is not static or fixed, that our position in the nature of things is not limited by any sense of restriction. There *is* something beyond the commonplace."[4] Charles Fillmore's experiences were beyond the commonplace. If he had not had them, he could not have proved to himself and others that with God all things are possible. Not some things, once in a while, but all things are possible for them who love the Lord. This was the committed faith that healed Charles and Myrtle. This was the faith that built Unity Village; this was the faith that led Charles into previously unexplored dimensions of Spirit.

When we were little, my brother and I loved to have Papa Charlie tell us the story of how one day when he was just a baby some Sioux Indians rode up to their cabin and took Charles from his mother's arms. They then jumped on their horses and rode away with him. She was desperate; she was all alone and had no idea where they were taking Charlie or if she would ever see her beloved son again. But she did. In the evening they brought him back to her and left as quietly and silently as they had come.

Charles always felt that perhaps they used him in one of their religious ceremonies and perhaps this is what started him on his spiritual quest. Not too long ago, I was telling this story to someone who was familiar with Native American mysticism, and he suggested another scenario. He suggested they took him for one of their ceremonies because they knew he was a soul with a special mission, and they wished to bless him on his way.

The cynic would probably say that I have romanticized my childhood and the people who were a part of it—especially my grandfather. Perhaps I have, but in all candor, I am unable to remember anything that wasn't good about him. It's not that I agreed with everything he taught or thought; but his absolute sincerity, integrity, and dedication were so far beyond anything I have seen in the world of religion that it is difficult not to idealize him. But, of course, that is the last thing he would have wanted; he enjoyed his humanity to the fullest, and his ego was so strong that it never had to be stroked or fed. The New Age prophets who insist on first-class tickets, stretch limos, and thousands of dollars to preach their gospels would have amused him.

I remember when my grandfather first decided to spend his winters in California; it was near the end of

World War II. At that time the hotels were filled with servicemen, and it was difficult to find rooms. A young couple who had a small apartment in Hollywood invited my grandfather and his second wife Cora to stay with them. I visited him there; it was a small place with two bedrooms and a combined living and dining room. The man was an artist for Disney Studios and had his palette and canvas set up in the middle of the living area. When I arrived, he was working and my grandfather was in the kitchen making a sandwich. I was impressed that with so little space this young couple still so generously shared it with Papa Charlie and his wife. My grandfather was very happy to be with them and stayed there until he found a home in Sherman Oaks.

Grandfather and Cora also had a farm that connected with Unity's property, and he lived there in the summers. When I visited him at his farm, he always had people staying with him who needed help temporarily. He never explained who they were or what the problem was. They would stay for a while and move on, and someone new would take their place.

Neither Charles and Myrtle nor their sons ever accumulated any personal wealth. Although they all lived well, everything was given back to their work. In 1892 Charles and Myrtle wrote a Dedication and Covenant that they adhered to as long as they lived, and their sons continued to honor their covenant. The covenant read: "We, Charles and Myrtle Fillmore, husband and wife, hereby dedicate ourselves, our time, our money, all we have and all we expect to have, to the Spirit of Truth, and through it, to the Society of Silent Unity. It being understood and agreed that the said Spirit of Truth shall render unto us an

Charles Fillmore—a man whose vision became reality.

equivalent for this dedication, in peace of mind, health of body, wisdom, understanding, love, life, and an abundant supply of all things necessary to meet every want without our making any of these things the object of our existence. In the presence of the Conscious Mind of Christ Jesus, this 7th day of December, 1892."

None of the family owned their homes; they all belonged to Unity. So if any of us left our jobs at the School, we also lost our home. My husband and I went to Florida in 1980 to work in the ministry for three years, and someone else moved into the home where I had spent most of my life. Since then, I have never again lived at Unity Village, although I did return to work there.

In the Bhagavad-Gita, Arjuna, the disciple, asks Krishna to tell him how he can recognize a man who knows the Truth; that is, how he can identify an illumined person. Krishna replies, "A man who is not affected by achievement or failure, who is free from emotions such as fear, anger, pride, vanity, jealousy, hate; a man who has disciplined his mind—he is wise; he is illumined."[5] This is a good description of my grandfather, the man I called Papa Charlie.

Top: Stanley Grace, friend, Rosemary, and her father, Rick
Fillmore, in the early '50s.

Bottom: Brothers Rick and Lowell Fillmore survey the
Village around 1960.

# 3. Rick Fillmore

As important as my grandfather was in my life, it was my father who was truly the pivotal person. The reason for this was that my mother was very ill for a number of years, and she passed away when I was just beginning high school. I spent much of my early life following my father as he transformed Unity Farm into Unity Village. Unity Village as it is today is the manifestation of his dream. It was his vision, his talent, and his imagination that created this unusual place.

After my father graduated from high school in Kansas City, he studied at the Chicago Art Institute and then spent a year traveling in Europe. While in Italy, he was impressed by the beautiful Italian Renaissance architecture. In England, he liked the warm charm of the lovely Cotswold cottages that dotted the English countryside. He decided to make the buildings that would house the Unity work a prototype of the Italian Renaissance architecture he so admired and make the homes in the mode of the English Cotswold cottages.

If ever there was a man who enjoyed his work, it certainly was my father. Unity Village today is a testament to his passionate dedication. There was nothing he liked more than showing visitors around the Farm. A day never passed that he didn't go to every nook and cranny where people were working.

In the beginning it was the Fillmores' desire to make Unity Village a self-reliant community. A lake was built for the water supply, gas and oil wells were drilled, orchards and vegetable gardens were planted. A dairy farm provided fresh milk, and chickens supplied eggs. The land provided limestone for the buildings, walks, and roads. Oak and walnut trees that were killed by the devastating 1930s drought were used to build cabinets and doors for the buildings. The Tower that was completed in 1929 held a large water tank that made a continuous supply of water possible.

Everything my father designed was not only beautiful but also had a utilitarian purpose. For instance, the lovely fountains in the front of the Administration Building also acted as its cooling system. He was one of the first people to use prefabrication in construction. The shortage of labor and materials caused by World War II brought progress to a halt, and he had to find new ways to build if work was to continue. He precast in concrete all of what is now the Administration Building and raised the finished molds into place. This was such an innovative way of building at that time that architects and builders came from all around the United States to see how it was done. And because the Fillmores had more faith than money, my dad helped unskilled workmen dis-

3

cover skills and even artistry they had no idea they possessed.

Engrossed as he was in building Unity Village, Rick Fillmore also found time to become actively involved in civic organizations in Kansas City. The members of these organizations enjoyed coming to Unity Farm for picnics, outdoor theater, and dances. He was president of the Kansas City Art Institute for a number of years. He also designed a lovely outdoor patio for Kansas City Repertory Theater, which was a part of the University of Missouri of Kansas City, UMKC. He was actively involved in helping create Kansas City's Starlight Theater, an outstanding facility in Swope Park, which presents outdoor plays and musicals during the summer.

Kansas City is the home of a number of people who have made important cultural contributions to twentieth-century America. Walt Disney began his career there. Joyce Hall, one of the cofounders of what is now Hallmark Cards, was a colleague of my father. Another was J. C. Nichols, the Kansas City developer who built one of the first—and surely one of the most beautiful—shopping centers in America and called it "The Country Club Plaza." Its spectacular Christmas lights are still seen in magazines and on TV. These men were visionaries, dedicated to turning a so-called "cow town" into a beautiful, exciting, sophisticated city.

My father had one friend who became a role model for me. Even today, whenever I feel tired, I think of her and how she refused to let age or even blindness dampen her creative spirit. Her name was Mary Hook. She was one of the first women architects in America. Mary built homes in Kansas City and developed Siesta Key in Sarasota, Florida. Her passion for building matched my dad's and they had a great time together. Mary lived until her 100th birthday, and I can truthfully say that I have never had a friend I admired more. When I first met her, she was probably in her eighties. She had a youthful, slender body, and her wise Buddha eyes and lovely white hair enhanced a face creased with a thousand wrinkles, giving her a beautiful, ageless quality.

My grandfather used to say, "We grow old because we think old thoughts." Both Mary and my grandfather proved that this is true. Both of them were eternally young because they remained excited about life. Even blindness could not suppress Mary's enthusiasm for building. She began to lose her eyesight as she moved into her nineties, and finally she was totally blind. For an artist and builder, this must have been particularly devastating. But she never complained. I remember visiting her a year or so before she died. When I asked how she was doing, she replied, "Well, in my mind I have been restoring some wonderful old buildings that I loved to visit when I was in Paris." She went on to say that even though she couldn't see outwardly she could visualize inwardly. Physically, her last days were spent in a nursing home in Kansas City, but mentally, she was in her beloved Paris restoring those buildings to their original splendor. This is not to say she didn't know exactly where she was; her mind was as sharp as could be. She just had the wonderful ability to not let physical circumstances keep her trapped.

I spent many happy times with Mary Hook, both in Kansas City and in Florida. Once she took me to a little house she had purchased in Hope Town, a village on the island of Great Abaco, one of the outer islands of the Bahamas. I met her at her home in Sarasota, where we packed her car and then drove across the state to Palm Beach. She was taking supplies from her house to a cargo ship that would deliver them to Hope Town. In Palm Beach, we checked into a hotel and some friends of mine took us to their home for dinner. Since they had a pool, they suggested that if we would like to swim to be sure to bring our suits. I shall never forget the expressions on their faces as Mary, all of 85 or 90 years of age, jumped on the diving board and did a perfect jackknife into the pool!

The next day when I awakened at the hotel, there was a note under the door from Mary, "It's six o'clock, and I'm going to the pier to load my things on the boat for Abaco." Hope Town was not an easy place to get to. We had to take a small prop plane across the Atlantic to a place called Marsh Harbor, and from there it was a twenty-minute boat ride to Hope Town. By the time we finally arrived, it was late afternoon, but Mary was still going strong. She hopped off the boat, took me to her home, and somehow found time to invite a group of her

Abaco friends for cocktails at seven o'clock. I was about thirty at that time, and I was exhausted, though I hadn't done nearly as much as this amazing woman had.

Another of my father's friends who had a profound influence on my life was Marcus Bach. Marcus was a spiritual researcher, lecturer and teacher, and the author of many books. He first came to Unity when he was writing a book about new American religions. When he and my dad met, they immediately recognized a spiritual kinship: both were great conversationalists, and both had minds that were alive with ideas and possibilities.

Marc traveled the world in search of people whose mystical experiences had led them into new dimensions. Nothing was beyond his interest; and when he spoke, whether he was telling of walking by the Ganges with a Hindu holy man or attending a voodoo ceremony in Haiti, you were there with him. He had been a teacher in the School of Religion at the University of Iowa. I thought how lucky his students were to have had such an exciting professor. As I sat in my father's living room and listened to Marc and my father converse, I was transported into new and mysterious worlds; it implanted in me the desire to see and experience for myself all those wonderful places Marc so vividly described.

There was something about my father's house that attracted interesting people. My dad had designed a living area that was especially comfortable. The house, as I said, was English Cotswold. The living and dining areas were both in one long room with a large stone fireplace at one end. The dining table was next to the fireplace. The living area was surrounded by windows on one side while the other side was filled with books in cases built into the wall. In the middle of the living room ceiling there was a beautiful wrought iron chandelier with electric candles, and a lovely mirror that my dad had built especially for the room hung between the dining and living areas. The house was simple, but warm and friendly.

Dad loved food and was himself a good cook. Helen, my father's housekeeper and my dear friend, was a cook to remember. Anyone who came to my father's house for dinner went away thinking, How did anyone make an apple pie taste like nectar of the god's? Good food, charming surroundings, and conversation that titillated the imagination made for evenings to remember.

After my father died and I married Ralph Rhea, we moved into my family home. I soon discovered that Ralph, just like my father, had the gift of attracting to Unity Village wonderful minds. Once again our living room embraced a flow of ideas from a remarkable eclectic group of visitors. Alan Watts, the sixties Zen guru, was the center of an evening I will never forget. Victor Frankl, the Austrian psychiatrist who wrote *Man's Search for Meaning*, was one of our special guests. Another was Carl Menninger from the world-renowned Menninger Clinic. We entertained Norman Vincent Peale, who credited Unity for helping him develop his positive philosophy and his perennial best-selling book *The Power of Positive Thinking*.

Steve Allen, one of America's best-known television personalities in the fifties and sixties, became a great friend of Ralph's. Steve at that time had a program called *Meeting of the Minds* on Public Television. The premise of the show was built on the idea of having historical characters from the past come together to discuss their thoughts about current and past events. Steve wanted Ralph to portray Will Rogers on the show. Unfortunately the program went off the air before Ralph could do it. It was easy to understand why Steve wanted Ralph for the part. He not only looked a great deal like Will Rogers, he also had the same dry wit.

One of my very favorite guests was Robert E. Lee, who with his partner Jerome Lawrence wrote so many wonderful plays: *Auntie Mame, Inherit the Wind, First Monday in October*, to name just a few. Bob Lee was one of the most intelligent, insightful men I have ever known. He was married to Janet Waldo Lee, a lovely, talented actress, and they shared a love that was so special everyone who knew them felt blessed by its radiance. Bob's gentle wisdom was expressed in the great lines of his plays, but it was also evident in the way he lived his life.

Most of the great souls who came to my father's house have moved into another dimension of living, but if the walls could talk, what fascinating conversations they could repeat! I wonder if those who live there now can feel the energy, the wonder of those sharp, enlightened minds.

After my great-grandmother died, our house became the gathering place for family celebrations. Nothing pleased my father more than planning holiday dinners. He loved to go to the grocery store to do the buying. When he returned, he would sound his horn, and Helen and I would run down the back stairs to help carry in bag after bag of special delicacies he had found for our holiday dinners. As I said, Helen was an unbelievably good cook, and my brother and I would eat so much that we would roll on the floor in distress after our holiday meals.

My grandfather was small in stature, but his sons were big men. They evidently took after their mother's family. My father had red hair, fair skin, and brown eyes, while my Uncle Lowell was blonde with blue eyes. They were very different in their temperaments and their lifestyles. My father had the soul of an artist, while my uncle was an esthetic who never ate meat but thoroughly enjoyed eating fruits and vegetables. His greatest pleasure was his garden, where he grew beautiful flowers. My Uncle Lowell was truly one of the world's innocents. I never heard him speak ill of anyone; he always sought the best in everyone, and he refused to ever give in to negation of any kind. Even though he was president of the School, every day he walked through the offices of Unity, visiting with the people who were working at their desks.

At Christmas, he donned a Santa Claus suit and handed out the Christmas presents.

Lowell's greatest joy was finding new ways to disseminate Unity's message to the world. It was by his insistence that Unity went into television. It was by his insistence that Unity literature was distributed around the world, that hospitals and prisons received free literature, and that radio broadcasts were never off the air. He wrote a regular column called "Things to Remember" for a magazine called *Weekly Unity*.[6] He was such a simple, gentle person that many people mistakenly thought of him as not too bright. But they were very wrong in their assessment of my uncle. His purity of spirit and his remarkable dedication to the principles of Truth were beyond the understanding of those who judged others by a more cosmopolitan standard.[7] Whenever I read about St. Francis of Assisi, I always think of my Uncle Lowell. They must have been very much alike.

Although my father and uncle were different, in many ways they were quite similar. Both were completely dedicated to the growth of Unity. Both were greatly influenced by their mother's early teachings. She had instilled in them moral principles that they faithfully adhered to all their lives. I have never known two men who had such unyielding integrity.

I remember one time when I was a young girl my father dropped me off at the movie theater. When he came to pick me up, I told him I was short a penny for my ticket but the lady let me in anyway. Although we were half way home, he turned the car around, drove back to the theater, and insisted I take a penny to the ticket seller. It may seem like a small incident, but I have never forgotten it. Even today, if I owe anyone any money at all, I want to take care of it immediately. They say character is revealed in small ways, and I believe this is true.

My grandmother was a member of the Women's Temperance League. My father would tell of how she would teach Uncle Lowell and him temperance songs to sing in front of saloons as the women walked back and forth with placards, proclaiming the evils of drinking. He said he would always remember this as one of the most embarrassing experiences of his childhood—especially since she dressed them in matching suits made from worn-out draperies that had hung in their living room! However, her feelings about alcohol must have made a lasting impression on her sons, for they never drank anything beyond a glass of wine, and that only on very special occasions.

My father was unable to accept my grandfather's decision to marry again after Myrtle's death. He felt this was disrespectful to his mother's memory. When my mother died, my father was only in his fifties, but he never remarried. He believed when you married, you married for life, and it was not possible for him to compromise on a principle that he felt strongly about. On one hand, he could be the most loving, understanding person in the world; on the other hand, he could be absolutely inflexible once he made up his mind about something.

However, my grandfather had the capacity to move forward on the path he felt was right for him without being swayed by the opinion of other people—even his sons, whom he loved very much. And so he married Cora Dedrick, who had for many years been both his and Myrtle's secretary. It was the right thing for him to do. Cora made his later years very happy ones. She helped him with his writing and was also a caring companion. After their marriage, they built a home on a wooded farm area that adjoined Unity Village. My father and Cora never became friends, but my grandfather and father had a remarkably close relationship.

There was never a Saturday night when my grandfather was in town that he didn't come to our house for dinner. Cora would bring him, and my father would take him home. My grandfather's marriage in no way diminished the respect, love, and deep admiration that both of his sons felt for him. It probably would have pleased him if my father could have learned to accept his marriage, but since he didn't, my grandfather wasn't going to let it change his relationship with either Cora or my father.

I became friends with Cora when she and Papa Charlie were living in California and I was in school there. She was a quiet, reserved lady who had studied modern dance. This was reflected in the way she moved and carried herself. She was a tall, slender woman with almost perfect posture. I developed a great respect for Cora and felt that my grandfather was fortunate to have such a devoted companion to share his later years.

My grandfather and I, as I have said, were very close; but one thing we disagreed on was, of all things, marriage—not his, but mine. He did not want me to get married. In fact, one time he wrote me a letter about a dream he had about me and my spiritual journey. In his dream, I was an Egyptian princess who had somehow failed to achieve my spiritual potential in my last life. I had instead chosen personal fulfillment. And so he said in this life experience I must put my spiritual journey ahead of personal attachments. Well, you can imagine how well that went over with an eighteen-year-old girl whose main desire in life was to find and marry her soul mate as quickly as possible!

A few months after receiving the letter about his dream I went to California to school. While there, I started dating the son of a Unity minister. We went out together almost every weekend, and my grandfather decided that he should alert my father before things got too serious. Lo and behold, I received an urgent letter from my dad, suggesting that as soon as the semester was over I should come home for a while. Papa Charlie had written that he was concerned about my future and felt I needed time away from my friend. This letter did not make me very happy with my grandfather or my father, but I dutifully went home for the summer.

As my grandfather and father hoped, absence did not make my heart grow fonder and my California romance dissolved quickly in the shallows of a fickle heart. I'm sure they heaved a sigh of relief, little knowing that my search for true love was not to be thwarted by a simple change in geography. In fact, I was pleased to be back home and away from a relationship that really wasn't that wonderful. To heal my bruised feelings and, of course, to work on my summer tan, I retreated to a place where I had always found solace, the swimming pool.

The pool did not fail me. One day I was lying in the sun by the sparkling water with my eyes closed when someone dove in the water close enough to splash it in my face. I sat up with a start and opened my eyes to hear my future husband apologizing profusely for getting me wet. I couldn't believe my eyes; before me was the answer to a young girl's prayer—a handsome, exciting, older man. I soon learned that he had just returned to civilian life from the army. The fact that he had never left the United States didn't dampen my appreciation of his bravery for serving his country. In fact, the blonde, curly-haired golden person who came out of the water epitomized all the attributes I was looking for in someone to share my life. It didn't take long for us to begin our courtship, which eventually led to marriage.

The amazing thing was that my father seemed very pleased about my choice. Instead of going back to California, I was remaining in Kansas City. He and my husband-to-be got along well, and I think my dad felt a sense of relief that I was going to marry someone who seemed more mature than most of the boys I had brought home. Also I would remain close by, and he would no longer have to worry about what I was going to do next.

The past years had been difficult for my father. My mother died just as I was entering my teens. My brother Charles was in college at the time and after graduating immediately went into the navy. He served as an officer on a minesweeper off the coast of New England. Our country was at war, and I know my dad spent many sleepless nights worrying not only about my brother's safety but also about how he was going to manage a headstrong teenage daughter all by himself. Things got even more complicated when my brother returned from service with a wife and baby daughter and no place to live. Until they could decide what work my brother was going to do and where he would do it, they moved into my father's home. Their arrival made our home a very busy place. My father's house could not comfortably accommodate five adults and a baby. My marriage would at least eliminate one person, and I would still be living nearby. So I was married with his blessings.

But my grandfather had an entirely different attitude. I think he was very disappointed in me. He didn't express his disappointment in words; it was rather his lack of enthusiasm that made me know he was far from pleased about it. He was in California when we were married, and he didn't come home for the wedding. I know he was not well at that time, but it hurt me that he was so detached from the whole thing when we had always been so close.

I never spent time with my grandfather after the wedding. When he finally returned from California, he was very ill and I was very pregnant. My son was born two months before his death. In retrospect, I feel that he thought, once again, I was choosing a path that would inhibit my spiritual enfoldment. And, since he was prophetic, he no doubt knew that this marriage had little chance for success because my husband's interests and mine were so dissimilar. Of course he was right, but at that time there was no way I would have listened to him. I am sure he realized that too.

Nevertheless, one beautiful afternoon in April 1947 I was married in my father's house. I married Stanley S. Grace. I was twenty-one years of age, with about as much knowledge of marriage as a twelve-year-old. My husband was thirty-six years old and a confirmed bachelor. But that day we were both completely unaware of what the future held. We blissfully made our vows and happily drove away to begin a life that was very different from what either one of us had ever known or imagined.

On my wedding day, my dad spent most of the time in the kitchen making hors d'oeuvres and crying. It was very difficult for him to see me leave his home. My brother Charles had not been back long and now I was leaving. After my mother's death and with my brother

away in World War II, Dad and I were completely depen-
dent upon each other for strength and courage. I can only
imagine how frightening it must have been for him to
have Charles, his only son, his pride and joy, somewhere
in the North Atlantic sweeping the sea for mines. When
you think of all the parents throughout centuries who
have had to sit home praying for their sons and daughters
who were far away fighting someone somewhere, it is a
tragic commentary on humankind's inability to settle differences in less painful and destructive ways.

But as I said before, at the time of my wedding, my
brother Charles was safely home and I could go without
guilt. My marriage did not in any way come between my
father and me. In fact, our bond grew even stronger with
the birth of my two children. There was no grandfather
ever more loving and caring of his grandchildren than my
father. A year or so after our marriage, Stanley and I bought
a farm that adjoined Unity Village, and there was never a
day that my dad didn't come and visit us or we didn't go to
visit him. He and my husband got along famously—in fact,
much better than my husband and I did!

The thing about parents that makes your relationship with them different from any other is that they love
you in a way that no one else ever does—at least good parents do. Of course they don't always behave the way we
would like. They make mistakes, act from their humanness, but when the chips are down, our parents will be
there when everyone else has gone. They love us through

our failures and our triumphs, in our joy and in our pain. A good parent's love is the nearest thing to unconditional love that we human beings can experience here on Earth.

I know that many, many people don't have this kind of parental acceptance, and I can only imagine how difficult it must be for those who do not have at least one caring parent. I know I have been richly blessed by having had a father like mine.

This is not to say that my father was perfect. He had the same human qualities we all have. He'd lose his temper and yell at us. He worried and was upset when we were late getting home. And, of course, I thought he was being unreasonably restrictive. He must have been disappointing to my brother at times, as he had little interest in sports or outdoor activities like fishing or hiking, which were the activities Charles especially enjoyed. My dad's interests were in the arts—painting, theater, and design. After he passed away, we found, locked in a closet in his studio on the seventh floor of the Unity Tower, paintings that none of us had ever seen or even known existed. He didn't consider himself a good artist, but many of the paintings, including a self-portrait, were excellent.

After dinner in the evening, my father would read the paper, listen to the news, watch some television; then when everyone had gone to bed, he would take out his sketchpad and draw late into the night. He also kept a journal, and each evening he wrote how the work had progressed that day. If something of personal importance happened, he would add a few lines about that.

Both he and my grandfather were night people. They stayed up late and rose late in the morning. My grandfather felt he could meditate best at night when the voices of the Earth became still.

When my dad was eighty years old, he took me on a trip to Europe. He had not been back since he had studied there in his youth. He said he wanted to show me the architecture and the beautiful galleries of Rome and Paris. At that time I was going through a particularly difficult period in my marriage, and I think he really thought it would be good for me to have some time away. I have always been grateful that we took that trip together because he died two years later.

Our journey began in Spain. We then traveled to Italy and, finally, to France. Sadly his health was failing, and he didn't have the stamina to walk through the museums he wished to visit, so he insisted that I do it for him. I know little about art, but I diligently wandered through every—or so it seemed to me—gallery in Madrid, Rome, Florence, and Paris. It made my father happy and me very tired. I wished, as I viewed some of the world's finest paintings, that my father was there to help me appreciate the intricacies and subtleties expressed by the brushes of those great artists.

My father had a wonderful day in France, visiting with a friend from America who had been sent by the Rockefeller Foundation to oversee the restoring of

Versailles. This charming man gave us a personal tour of this magnificent place and took my father to his private studio, where they spent several hours discussing art. I think that day was the best day of our trip for my dad.

My favorite time was in Southern Italy, even though I had a scare there. We spent a night in a beautiful, old hotel in Sorrento and in the morning took a boat to the island of Capri. My father had been there some sixty years before and had fallen in love with it. When we arrived there, he had a cold and was not feeling well; nevertheless, he was glad to be back and insisted that I go out and enjoy the day. I eagerly followed his instructions and spent several hours just wandering up and down streets, pausing here and there to admire the lovely view and to observe the multicultural tourists who daily invaded the island.

When I finally returned to our hotel suite, I found blood spots on the carpet of our sitting room. I rushed into my father's bedroom, afraid of what I might find. What I found was my dad sitting on his bed, woefully trying to stop his toe from bleeding. It seemed that while he had been trimming his toenails he had cut his toe. In his later years he had developed diabetes, and any injury, even a very small one, caused him to bleed profusely. We soon stopped the bleeding, but cutting his toe plus having a cold was not how he had intended to spend his time in Capri.

I shall never forget my father's face as he turned to me with tears in his eyes and said: "You know the most difficult thing about growing old is that inside you are still young: there is still the desire to run through the fields, to dance into the night, to see and to do all those things that are possible when you are young. But when the spirit is trapped in a tired body, a body that just wants to be left alone, it is very frustrating." He then smiled and shook his head gently. "Well," he went on to say, "I guess I'll just have to get a new body, but that is sad, too, because this one has served me so well."

My father believed in reincarnation and swore he could remember his past life very clearly. He believed he was a very young soldier in the Civil War and was killed on the battlefield. After he was shot, he did not realize that he was dead and he wandered around trying to get people to talk to him. He couldn't understand why no one would acknowledge his presence.

A couple of years after our trip, my father suffered a mild stroke. As he was recovering from it, somehow he injured his leg. The wound would not heal because of his diabetes, and it became infected. Eventually he had to be hospitalized, a thing he really resisted. He had great distrust of hospitals and doctors, and as it worked out, his distrust was not misplaced.

I shall never forget the day that a doctor walked into my father's hospital room with a group of medical students closely following him. Without any compassion for my father's feelings, the doctor pulled back the sheet, told the students to gather closer so that they could see my father's wound, and then explained that it was gangrenous and the limb would have to be amputated! He then pulled the sheet back up to cover the leg and left with the cowering young interns right behind him. He treated my father as a case study. There was no feeling, no understanding of what his pronouncement, "The leg must be removed," meant to my father. It was all I could do to keep from running after him, shouting how utterly insensitive it was to treat a fellow human being in such a cold, uncaring way.

I never saw that doctor again, and the leg didn't come off. My father refused to have the surgery and insisted on going home. He said he would either be healed through prayer, or he would move on. There was no hesitancy in his decision. I've often wondered if my father might have made a different choice if the doctor had taken the time to treat him as a person rather than an infected leg that must be removed. But he didn't, so we took my father home to his beloved Unity Village.

His leg didn't heal, and he blamed himself. He felt his faith was not as strong as it should have been. I disagreed with him, because he had tremendous faith. His faith had created a place of beauty, of peace, of inspiration. His faith had given him the courage to go on after he lost the woman he loved. His faith had given him the ability to be a wonderful father and grandfather. His faith had given him the integrity and strength to always uphold those principles in which he so firmly believed. I do not think it was lack of faith that kept his leg from healing; rather, it was his resistance to living without the energy and freedom to move forward in building his "New Jerusalem."

He told me as he was coming to the end of his journey here that he was living in two worlds. Part of him, he said, was still there with me and part "was already on the other side." He admonished me not to be concerned as he was going forward into another dimension of living. He said those who had gone before were already with him, and his transition would be easy and beautiful. He went on to tell me that all his life he had thought that things were either black or white, right or wrong, but he was learning that this is not true. He was finally realizing that there was no black or white, only shades of gray which are given color and definition through our individual perception and understanding.

My brother was on a trip to Europe with a Unity tour when our father became so very ill, and my dad said he had to stay alive till Charles returned so he could tell him good-bye. That is exactly what he did. Charles returned one day, and my dad made his transition a day or so later.

I thought I would feel very much alone when he was gone, but instead I had a sense of peace. I felt I hadn't really lost him, that he was still with me and had just moved into a different space. That space was invisible, but nevertheless very real. I could see him free of the physical restrictions that had so frustrated him, and I knew that wherever he was his fine, creative mind was already visualizing a new City of God. In fact, he told me a day or so before he left that he was already planning how he would find a way to build his New Jerusalem.

"And I saw the holy city, the new Jerusalem, coming down out of heaven from God, prepared as a bride adorned for her husband" (Rev. 21:2).

Rosemary's mother, Harriet Fillmore, as the "Grand Duchess" in the 1930s, when Rick was president of the Kansas City Art Institute.

# 4. My Mother

I should remember my mother better than I do. I was in my early teens when she died, but mostly I just remember her long and painful illness.

I know very little about her early life and have no knowledge at all of who Harriet really was as a person. I do not know what she hoped and dreamed or how she felt about Unity and her life at the Farm. I have always guessed that it must have been difficult for the women who married into our family. Every one of the Fillmore men was so passionately involved in pursuing their collective dream that if his wife was not able to share that passion it would have been very easy to feel left out.

My parents met when my mother came to work for Unity, then located in Kansas City. Her father had migrated to the United States from Ireland during the potato famine. He settled in Edgerton, Kansas, a little town just west of Kansas City. My mother's maiden name was Collins, and she was one of seven children. Her parents were gone before I was born. Her brothers and sisters moved to various parts of the country, and only one sister besides my mother remained in Kansas City.

I do know my mother enjoyed people. She liked parties and traveling and was especially happy when my father was participating in Kansas City social activities. I have a lovely picture of her in a beautiful ball gown that she wore to a Beaux Arts Ball that was given when my father was president of the Kansas City Art Institute.

She contributed to the growth of Unity Village by starting the first Unity Sunday school, which was held in the Silent Unity Chapel. She planned picnics and parties for the workers and their children.

My mother was a small, pretty woman with hazel eyes and golden blonde hair. That was absolutely the opposite of me. I was always tall for my age, had very dark brown hair, and was a skinny, gawky kid. When I looked at her, I would lament to myself how disappointing it was that I didn't look more like my little mother.

When I was twelve years old, she became ill and had her first operation. The Fillmores were all wary of hospitals and doctors since their past experiences had been so negative. I don't know what my mother felt about the medical profession, but she did bravely entrust herself to their care. After her first operation, she improved for a while, but then the pain returned and she was told that it was necessary for her to go back for another operation. At that time there was no chemotherapy or radiation—you had to rely on the surgeon's knife. She never fully recovered from the second surgery; however, she continued to explore every option that might help her—healers, diets, medicine—but to no avail.

It was a sad time for our family. I couldn't understand why she had to suffer so much pain, and I kept asking God why this was happening to my mother. I was frightened and angry. It didn't seem fair that I was losing her when I needed her most. There were so many things I wanted to talk to her about—things that girls can only share with their mothers. And although our family doctor had tried to prepare us for her death, I still kept hoping for a miracle. When you are young, death is something that happens to someone else. It doesn't happen to you or your family; it happens to other people. But it happened to us.

I shall never forget the day she died. It was a bleak January day. I was in gym class playing basketball when the principal came into the room and said we should stop playing for a moment because she needed to speak to our teacher. She whispered something into the gym teacher's ear; they both then turned and looked at me with sympathetic concern. I knew something bad had happened even before the teacher told me to change into my street clothes, that someone had come to take me home.

Mr. Lucky, my dear good friend, was waiting in the car for me. My school was about three miles from the farm, and we made the trip in absolute silence; I didn't ask him what had happened—I just sat quietly trying not to cry.

My mother had been extremely ill all through the Christmas holidays. Our usual Christmas celebration did not happen. My father's expenditures had become so great with my mother's illness and a son in college that our presents were limited to one per person. The strange thing is that I can remember my present that year, much more vividly than any I received before or after. It was a little red shirt that Helen, our wonderful housekeeper, had made for me.

The doctor had told my father that my mother was getting weaker and weaker and could not be expected to live much longer. She slipped in and out of consciousness and most of the time did not recognize us. But she remained alive throughout the holiday, and it became time for my brother to return to the university.

It must have been really tough for him to go back to school when his mother was barely clinging to life. She and Charles were very close, and as the war in Europe rapidly began to escalate, she became fearful that he would be called into service. She was gone before this occurred, but with a mother's intuition she saw it happening and, of course, it did.

Charles went back to college, and I returned to high school. One of my mother's sisters came from California to be with her, and we also had nurses in our home around the clock. It was a miserable time. Helen kept everything going. She, my aunt, and I shared the one upstairs bedroom. My mother had been moved to my room, and the nurse had my brother's room. My father didn't know where to go or what to do: the house was filled with women, and his wife was drifting away. I don't know if he could have handled it if he hadn't had my grandfather's faith to draw upon when his own wavered. The Fillmores believed so strongly in healing; it was difficult for my father to understand why it wasn't working for his beloved wife.

When I arrived home on that cold, gray day in January, the person who greeted me at the door was Dr. Miller, our family doctor. My father had been in Kansas City at the Unity office and was not yet home. This dear, sweet man had stayed to comfort me until my father returned. My mother had many specialists during her illness, but through it all Dr. Miller remained steadfast. He was there in the beginning and in the end. He was the kind of doctor everyone dreams of having but can rarely find in medicine today. Dr. Miller understood that we are more than broken bones or bad stomachs, and his loving attention cured more illnesses than any pill ever could.

If we were to make a list of important things we have lost as we have moved forward with ever more sophisticated medical technology, I would put right at the top "family doctors," doctors who were with you throughout your life. They knew your family, your history, your children, and your children's children. They were your friends, your confidants, and they cared. You could call them night or day, which I did when my children were small. They would patiently listen and, if necessary, come to your home. These were wonderful men and women, and anyone who was lucky enough to have had a family physician like Dr. Miller should be eternally grateful. I know I am.

Dr. Miller was not only with me when my mother died. Years and years later he was there taking care of my father after his unfortunate experience with that cold, orthopedic surgeon. The difference between those two doctors was so great that it is hard to realize they were in the same profession.

My father was devastated by my mother's death. We all knew that it was good that she was finally released from the pain of her illness, but on the other hand, he had lost his wife and Charles and I had lost our mother.

My mother had not wanted to be cremated as all of the Fillmores had been. She requested that she be buried somewhere close so that we could visit her grave. My Aunt Alice, Uncle Lowell's wife, made the same request. It seems that the wives of my father and uncle didn't completely embrace their husbands' theology.

Since it had been my mother's desire to have a traditional funeral and burial, it became necessary to find suitable clothes for her to wear. She had lost so much weight during the last months of her illness that her own clothes were much too large. My Aunt Eleanor from California decided I should go to Kansas City with her to find a shroud—a garment for my mother to be buried in.

I did not like my Aunt Eleanor very much. I had not known her before she came to be with my mother, and I found her presence intrusive. Also, her relationship with my father was strained, and I think my father and I were both looking forward to her departure. But I dutifully went with her. I had no idea what a shroud was or how you chose something for your mother's funeral.

I felt I was in a bad dream that wouldn't stop. I remember standing with my aunt in a dimly lit department store, watching as a salesperson began showing us what looked to me like negligees. My aunt kept prodding me to choose one as she and the saleslady discussed the pros and cons of each gown. I had no idea which one was right, and I couldn't believe they were expecting me to make such a decision. Finally, I pointed to one of them and prayed that my aunt would be satisfied and we could leave as quickly as possible.

This experience must have sufficiently traumatized me, because after standing in that store I have no memory of the funeral or the graveside service. I don't know who was there, what was said, or what happened afterwards. I only remember looking at those gowns, and thinking, What possible difference does it make which one we choose? My mother was gone, and they shouldn't care about the color and fabric. Didn't they understand that none of that mattered? My mother wasn't here anymore; she was gone.

Everyone left a few days after the funeral. Charles returned to school and Aunt Eleanor to California; the house that had seemed too small now felt too large and empty. Only my father, Helen, and I remained. I don't know what my dad and I would have done without Helen.

She ran the house, cooked our meals, saw that I got off to school, and was there when I got home. She was the rock, the anchor that kept us from sliding into disarray.

Helen Davis had come to work for my family when she was just eighteen. She was living with her family on a farm in southern Missouri when she answered an ad my mother had placed in the newspaper. I have always marveled at her bravery in getting on a bus and traveling to Kansas City to work for people she had never seen and knew nothing about. It must have been very scary for her. She had never been away from her family nor had she traveled very far from the little town where she had lived all her life.

I was three when she came to live at our house, and I shall forever be grateful to God for bringing us together. She became my second mother, my sister, my confidant, and my caretaker. I cannot remember when she was not there.

My father taught her to cook, and it wasn't long until she became a gourmet chef. He was always encouraging her to try new recipes: soon she was preparing international cuisine, everything from sukiyaki to sauerbraten, and it was always delicious. I can honestly say that her pies were the best I have ever eaten, and her southern fried chicken was without equal. She had never heard of Unity before her arrival at the farm, but very quickly she became involved in the Sunday school, and soon the Unity philosophy became an important part of her life. Even today in her nineties she never fails to attend the Women of Unity meetings and was for many years their president.

Helen watched over me when I was a little girl. As I grew older she became my best friend. Together we enjoyed all the activities the farm afforded. We went swimming in the summer, ice-skating in the winter. We took long walks in the fall, and we never missed a Saturday dance or a Sunday band concert. When I got married and had children of my own, she was as caring as any doting grandmother.

I have been asked if I believe in angels, and I always say yes without equivocation. However, my angels are not heavenly beings who hover in the invisible. My angels are real flesh-and-blood human beings who always appear when they are needed. Some stay for a moment and others a lifetime. Helen has been my lifetime angel. She had to have been sent to Unity Farm and my family by divine appointment. She has blessed our lives in ways that any celestial spirit would find difficult to equal. I truly don't know how we would have been able to move through my mother's illness and death without her. She provided the sustenance, the continuity that kept some sense of normalcy in our very unsettled household.

When I visit Helen in the retirement home where she now resides, she often muses on what gave her the courage to answer that little want ad. She had a job teaching in a small rural school, and there was no compelling circumstance that made it necessary for her to leave her family and friends. She says for some reason she just felt that it was very important that she answer my mother's ad.

After my father's death, Helen worked for a while in the Unity offices and then became the hostess of the Unity Country Club, where she stayed until her retirement. She was an integral part of our family and also of the growth of Unity Farm.

Each person who was led to Unity in its beginning years played a vital role in its development. The fabric of life is woven of individual threads, and the pattern would not be complete without the contribution of each thread. When I think back on my childhood, I'm even more convinced that some benevolent energy was like a magnet, drawing just the right souls needed to create that place that we called Unity Farm.

I shall always regret the loss of my mother. I wish I could have known her better, but I'm not sure if we ever really know our parents, even if they live to be one hundred. It is almost impossible for us to view our parents objectively, even when we are adults. Somewhere the little child in us never stops seeking the love and approval of the two people who were the center of our early years, and it is very difficult for that child to see his or her parents as individuals who have their own soul needs.

Why some people are healed and others are not is a question only God can answer. We have learned something about the evolutionary process, but we still do not understand why bad things happen to good people. I am convinced that there is meaning in everything that happens to us. What seems terrible at the time it is happening always has a purpose hidden somewhere in the experience which contributes in some way to our growth. I like to think that what my mother suffered brought her greater strength and greater understanding as she moved forward on her journey.

When my first grandson was born, my daughter chose to call him Jacob. She said the name just came to her, and I was reminded of Jacob wrestling with the angel who would not let him go until he had blessed him. Immediately I thought of my mother. It was as if she were reaching through veils of time to assure me that she had found God's blessing in the illness she had so valiantly fought. I pray that this is true.

Young friends: Charles R. and Frances in the late 1920s.

# 5. The Third Generation—
## Charles, Frances and I

My brother Charles, my cousin Frances, and I grew up together at Unity Farm. Frances was the child of my father's brother Royal. Her mother had died just after she was born, and her father as well when she was two years old. She would spend her summers with her mother's family in Ohio but would return in the fall to go to school in Lee's Summit. Since she and Charles were the same age, they shared many friends and have maintained a close relationship throughout the years.

Although I was four years younger than Fran, as we call her, she was like a sister to me; and we spent many happy days together conjuring up glamorous make-believe lives that were lived on the French Riviera or as film stars in Hollywood. Our child minds could turn the Silent Unity Building into a castle in Monaco and the Unity Inn into a villa whose terrace looked to the Mediterranean Sea. We were both romantics, and our fantasy always included a handsome prince who would rescue us from some dire misfortune.

Fran, always a pretty child, grew into a beautiful teenager and attracted beaus like flies to honey. She was sweet and kind to me and would eagerly share what was going on in her life. I, of course, took vicarious pleasure as she confided her feelings about some new beau. In retrospect, I marvel at what an amazing person my cousin is. She grew up without a mother and father. Her childhood was spent with uncles and aunts—her winters at Unity Farm and her summers with her Ohio relatives, who usually took her to their home in Cape Cod. Her uncle was president of Frigidaire, and his family's lifestyle was far more elegant than anything she experienced with us. We used to kid Fran that it took two months for her to come back down to earth after mingling with the rich and famous. But the truth is that Fran had the wonderful ability to be happy wherever she was. Being shuttled between families whose interests and approach to life were so diverse would have been challenging to any child, but Fran somehow remained centered. If she felt confused or unhappy at times, she didn't express it to those who cared for her. She was and is a remarkable person.

After graduating from college, Fran went to Dayton to take a job in radio. While there, she met and married an executive with General Motors, Robert Lakin. They had three children, two boys and a girl. Fran relished her role as wife, mother, and homemaker. She created for her children the kind of life she must have longed for when she was a child.

Fran came back to Unity Village to visit, but after her marriage and the birth of her children, she slowly released her ties to Unity. Today she and her grown children are very involved in the charismatic church. It was difficult for me to understand how she could embrace a theology that is so different from the one that she had known as a child, but she finds great solace in her church, and I am happy for her. Each of us has our own path, and if there is one thing in life I have learned, it is that we must free one another to follow our individual soul's need. I'm deeply grateful that Fran has been a part of my life. Although she lives in the Northeast and I am in Jamaica and we are not often together, she is very much in my heart and mind and we always keep in touch by phone.

My brother Charles and I have had a very complex relationship. I had a real hero worship of my brother when I was young, but he also had the capacity to make me so angry that I wanted to literally fight him, and fight we did.[8] After having a boy and girl of my own, it became very clear that brothers and sisters take great joy in irritating one another. Charles, when we were kids, knew exactly which button to push to upset me. And when he pushed it, without fail, I reacted—just as I'm sure he knew I would.

Sibling relationships are multifarious. On one hand, our brothers and sisters are enormously important in shaping who we are. On the other hand, there can be vast differences in personalities, which seem to belie any relationship at all. To me, my brother was everything I was not. Four years older, he was smart, good-looking, and had lots of friends—and most of all, he was a boy. It was my observation that boys got to do more, got away with more, and were more respected in the chauvinistic society that prevailed at that time. For this reason, I believe I was always jealous of my brother. It wasn't that I had any desire to *be* a boy, I just felt he was awarded opportunities that were not available to me.

And I think my presence was a constant source of irritation to him, because I was always someone who either had to be looked after or avoided. When you are a boy, the last thing you want is a little sister tagging after you or telling your parents what you did or didn't do to or for her. By the time I started high school, Charles was already in college. And when I began college he was in the navy. So after our childhood, when we were both living at home, our paths really didn't come together again until he returned to Unity after his tenure in the service—a long gap.

Charles and Fran seemed to do everything right. They went to the right schools, joined the right sororities and fraternities, married the right people, and never divorced. And then there was me. Somehow I always found it hard to follow the path they had skipped down so easily.

For instance, in high school Fran was a beauty queen with many handsome suitors at her beck and call. When I was in high school I had only one boyfriend—a tall, skinny kid who played piano. We began going together when I was a sophomore and remained fast friends until he returned from the army after serving in

World War II. I thought he was the greatest piano player since Gershwin. I would take him to family parties at my Aunt Alice's and Uncle Lowell's because they had a piano. After dinner he would play boogie-woogie as my family sat quietly praying that we would soon go away. Boogie was not their idea of after-dinner music, but they were polite if not impressed.

Fran went to Stephens College, at that time an all-girls' school in Columbia, Missouri, and loved it. I went to Christian College, an all-girls' school in Columbia, Missouri, and was miserable. After Stephens, Fran spent her last two college years at the University of Iowa. There she joined the Kappa Kappa Gamma Sorority and found time to fall in love two or three times.

Charles attended the University of Missouri, majored in journalism, became a Beta Theta Phi, and was voted by the sorority girls the man they would most like to be stranded with on a desert island! After graduating, he went to Midshipman School and became a naval officer. I was much impressed by the ability of both Fran and Charles to be so successful in school. And I was particularly proud of my brother, since the girls seemed to consider him a real hunk.

After I attended Christian College, it was decided that I should go to the University of Kansas. By this time Charles had married his high school sweetheart, Anne Jones, while still in the navy. She had graduated from KU and was also a Kappa Kappa Gamma. I said I would go, but my heart wasn't in it. What I really wanted to do was attend the Pasadena Playhouse School of Theater in California. But my family thought I should go to a university, so I packed my bags and attended sorority rush week with the idea firmly planted in my mind that I must be accepted into the Kappa Kappa Gamma Sorority or I would disgrace the family name. No one told me this, of course; it was my own perception.

When I arrived on campus and was assigned to my room, I sensed that this was not going to be a happy experience. My roommate turned out to be the daughter of the managing editor of one of the major newspapers in the Midwest. She placed pictures of foreign correspondents, who she intimated were friends or former lovers, strategically around the room. Our phone never stopped ringing, bringing invitations from every sorority on campus requesting her presence at various functions. Always shy, I didn't just fade into the woodwork, I *was* the woodwork. I could think of nothing to say at the few parties I was invited to attend, and the Kappas certainly didn't seem to know I existed—hardly surprising, as I wasn't sure myself! My roommate was rushed by all the top sororities, each one trying to get her to "spike"—commit to joining their group before the end of rush week—according to her.

The only calls I received were from my concerned family, wanting to know how things were going. Each day became bleaker than the last. I was beginning to think that not only were the Kappas not going to want me but I would be lucky to be allowed into a student dorm. But God is good and one night right in the middle of rush week I went out to dinner and ate something that made me very, very ill. I developed a severe case of food poisoning. I was so ill that my family had to come and take me home. There my illness proved so debilitating that several weeks passed before I regained my strength. By that time rush week was long over and school was well into the first semester. If I were to go to KU, I would have to wait till midterm. Instead I got on a train and headed for California to enroll at the Pasadena Playhouse. I was very relieved and very happy. I didn't like getting sick, but a few weeks in bed was a lot better than spending two years in a school where I knew I just didn't fit. Psychologists, even metaphysicists, might say I subconsciously brought the illness on myself. Whether I did or didn't, one thing was obvious: I did not belong in a sorority. I did enjoy my year at the Playhouse, and I probably should have gone back instead of getting married; but then I wouldn't have had my beautiful children, and my life would have taken a different course.

It is my belief that we make soul choices that are necessary for our enfoldment; and if at times we wander away, there is a guiding thread that keeps pulling us back to the path that destiny has marked for us. My golden thread is Unity. It is as much a part of me as my heartbeat or as my breathing, and I think this is equally true for my brother. In some way both of us are attached by an invis-

ible umbilical cord to this indefinable spiritual abstraction
we call Unity. It is the energy that has propelled our lives.
And, although we have struggled with it and with each
other over it, it has been and always will be in this life
experience a bond that my brother and I share. Neither of
us, I think, quite understands why, but we nevertheless
know that we were given something very precious to
nourish and cherish.

Our ways have been different, but our inspiration
was from the same source. Charles is a realist and a prag-
matist—I'm an idealist, a dreamer. He is left-brained, I am
right-brained. He is a conservative, a Missouri "good ole
boy," happiest when he is with his fishing and hunting
buddies or walking through the woods with his dogs.
There is nothing pretentious or grandiose about my
brother. In fact, he shies away from those who project this
image. He has always been particularly wary of people
who use their spirituality to impress others with how
much more enlightened they are than most mortals.
However, his rather self-effacing attitude hides a very
competitive spirit that is not easily duped or led down
paths he does not wish to walk.

During his tenure as president, Unity School
enjoyed its most prosperous years. He made James Dillet
Freeman executive vice-president and Otto Arni treasurer. Both of these men grew up in Unity: James in Silent
Unity under the tutelage of May Rowland, and Otto
worked closely with my dad, overseeing Unity Village.

Both of these men loved Unity just as Charles and I do and were completely dedicated to its growth. Charles was a good chief executive officer. He knew the value of hiring dedicated, creative people and then trusting them to run their own departments.

In the '60s and '70s Unity was an exciting place to work. Sig and Jane Paulson were ministers at the Unity Village Chapel, and hundreds upon hundreds of people came to their Sunday services. My husband Ralph Rhea and I produced "The Word" which was heard and seen on over a thousand radio and television stations. These one-minute programs featured well-known celebrities giving a "Unity Thought for the Day." At that time the Unity Village Activities Center, which was built after Charles became president, became the center for seminars and lectures featuring some of the best writers, scientists, and theologians of that era.

Charles was open to new ideas, and once he made up his mind that your proposal was good for Unity, he gave you the freedom to bring it into fruition. I'm sure if we had been bogged down with committees, management teams, and so on, we could never have produced "The Word." Instead, we developed our own film crew and with a very small staff had truly miraculous results. Ralph and I were invited to attend broadcasting conventions around the country to explain how we successfully obtained so much free public service time for our one-minute program. I have always felt that we were successful because Charles gave us the creative freedom to produce "The Word" in the way we thought best.

Soon after we were married, Ralph joined me as co-director of the Radio and Television Department. It was a wonderful time in my life. I was happily married to a man I loved and admired, and our partnership also encompassed our work. Ralph had spent most of his life in Unity. He was a man of many talents: he had been a successful minister, was a wonderful speaker and teacher, and an excellent writer. He had a great sense of humor, and I have never known anyone who could make me laugh as Ralph did. It was Ralph who wrote all the scripts for "The Word,"[9] and eventually he had two books published—one by Hawthorne, *The Word Is ...*, and one by Hallmark, *The Good Word*. It was one of those magical periods in life when everything came together in perfect unison.

This lovely time came to an abrupt halt when my brother and I became embroiled in a battle of wills that ended with me leaving Unity School in 1980. Ralph and I then moved to Florida where we served in two ministries: one in Delray Beach with our dear friend Mary Kupferle and then in Port Richey. Ralph became ill while we were in Port Richey so we returned to Kansas City. Upon our return, I began the Unity Myrtle Fillmore Center. It was a challenging time. Ralph's health continued to fail. Beginning a ministry with scant financial resources in an area where there was already an abundance of fine Unity churches proved to be an uphill climb. It would not have been possible for the center to survive if it had not been for the loving emotional and spiritual support Ralph and I received from our family and our many Unity friends and teachers.

Ralph passed away in 1986, just as we were moving the center into a new location. I was devastated. I had not only lost my dear husband and my best friend, I also no longer had the wisdom he had garnered in fifty years of successful ministry to guide and direct me. However, I felt I owed it to the wonderful people who attended our little church to keep things on schedule. And, no doubt, it was having to meet deadlines that made it possible for me to move through this very difficult period. The loving people who were part of our ministry gave me the strength to continue.

One day, a couple of years after Ralph's passing, my brother came to visit me at the Myrtle Fillmore Center. His visit was brief, but he left a letter with me inviting me to return to Unity School. I gratefully accepted his invitation because Unity Village was my home and being separated from it had been very painful. Duke Tufty, a bright young graduate minister, took over my ministry, and I returned to Unity School, working as a member of the Retreat Department and as a traveling lecturer. Slowly, my brother and I healed our differences, and today we are closer than we have ever been.

Charles has been my nemesis and my savior. He has been my rock and my hard place. He has stood up for me when I'm sure he would rather have given me a kick in the pants. But he has been there when I needed him. I don't know what my life would have been without my brother, but I do know that he has played a major role in its enfoldment. And even when we were poles apart, I never stopped loving him.

Our lives have run parallel to each other. However, his has been a straight and steady course, while mine diverted into tributaries before returning to the main flow. We both have spent our entire working careers in Unity, starting with summer jobs as teenagers. He has been married for some fifty years to the same woman and has two daughters, Harriet DeBauge and Connie Bazzy. Connie is now Chairperson of Unity School's new Board of Directors. I was married twice and also have two children, a son and a daughter by my first husband. My son, Rick Grace, worked for Unity School for a number of years before leaving to establish his own business. My daughter, Rosalind Tanner, followed her great-grandmother's interests by pursuing a career in helping children through special education and as a clinical social worker. She is now a practicing psychotherapist. Charles and I also have two grandchildren each; his are two girls and mine are two boys.

Charles has never lived away from Unity Village since his return from the navy. I lived a year in California, working with Sue Sikking in Unity by the Sea in Santa Monica, then three years in Florida ministries, eight years in Kansas City with the Myrtle Fillmore Center, and then four years in Jamaica associated with Unity Faith Center in Montego Bay. It is comforting to know that my brother is at Unity Village when I am far away, and I pray that he will always be there.

Even as a child, I had a desire to know about far-away places. I remember when I was very young someone told me that if you dug straight through the Earth you would come out in China. I decided that I would start digging. I spent days with my little shovel trying to get to China, and I was extremely disappointed when I realized I just wasn't going to make it. It wasn't until I was in my early thirties that I finally got to Asia when I was on a trip that took me around the world and changed my life.

Top: Rosemary and the Queen of Thailand.
Bottom: Rosemary with Indian Prime Minister Nehru
(both photos 1962).

# 6. The Trip

I think I probably inherited my wanderlust from my grandfather, because the rest of our family seemed perfectly content to stay at Unity Village and had little or no desire to travel the world. I was different. Although I loved Unity Village, I always wanted to see what was "out there." I wanted to experience different people, different cultures, and different religions. I wanted to listen to strange voices and feel other rhythms. I felt as though I were waiting for a summons to all those places I had never seen.

When the summons came, in the shape of an offered opportunity for a trip, I answered it eagerly, even though it meant leaving my family for forty days. It was the most memorable experience of my life. For a while I became a part of places I had only heard existed and of worlds I had no idea existed. I met people who became a part of history and people who have dissolved into time.

The trip was organized by the People-to-People Program. This organization was started by Joyce Hall of Hallmark cards after World War II. The idea was inspired by President Eisenhower, who became the honorary chairman. President Eisenhower felt the best way to ensure that the world would never again have a world war was for people to get to really know one another through exchange programs, travel, and correspondence. It was created with the premise that the more we know and understand one another, the less likely we are to want to destroy one another.

I became involved with the People-to-People Program soon after its inception. *Daily Word* was also on television at that time with a syndicated program that was seen in eighty markets. Because of my involvement with People-to-People and the television program, I was invited to join a small group of women in the media to present People-to-People plaques to the Heads of State in countries around the world to encourage them to participate in the program.

The time was the early sixties, John F. Kennedy was President, and America was just beginning to become involved in the conflict in Vietnam. It was a pivotal moment in the history of humankind. The world leaders were an eclectic group; some were at the end of their tenure and others were just starting to explore their power. In some countries, we were successful in having time with these leaders, and in others we failed to gain an audience. Besides participating in the People-to-People Program, I took with me a cinematographer to shoot footage to include on the *Daily Word* program and also to make a half-hour movie, *Around the World in Search of Faith*, which Unity would produce for public service use on television.

The first stop on our forty-day journey was Japan. Here we failed to meet the emperor, but for me it was an especially interesting experience because a few months before my trip, Marcus Bach had brought a group of Japanese religious leaders to Unity Village. Marc had spent some time in Japan after the Second World War. It was his desire to bring these Japanese gentlemen to America to help heal the spiritual wounds left from the war and, in particular, the bombing of Hiroshima.

Before coming to Unity Village, Marc had called and asked me to try to set up a meeting with former President Harry Truman, who was then residing at his longtime home in Independence, Missouri. Marc had hoped that if these men met with former President Truman, they would have a time of reconciliation. I had explained to Marc that I would try, but that my record with the Trumans was not too good!

When my brother was at the University of Missouri, one of his good friends was Margaret Truman's best friend in Independence, Missouri. When Truman was President, he made his home in Independence his summer White House. To make a long story as short as possible, one summer afternoon when I was about fourteen years old, I was home alone. I had just washed my hair and was putting it up on curlers when there was a knock at the door. When I answered, I discovered it was my brother's friend Mary Shaw, who was known as Shawzie. I told her Charles was unfortunately gone for the day but asked if I could give him a message.

She explained that Margaret Truman, the daughter of the President of the United States, was waiting in our driveway and she wanted a membership to the Unity Country Club so that she could use the swimming pool when she was in Independence. It seemed that the other country clubs in the vicinity were so busy that they could not offer her any privacy.

I answered, with all the dignity I could muster while having half of my hair in curlers and the other half soaking wet, that no one could have a Unity Country Club membership unless that person worked for Unity School, because it was built for the Unity employees; but if she wanted to go swimming, I would be happy to sign up for her anytime she wanted to come over—of course, it would cost her twenty-five cents.

I thought I was handling the situation pretty well. However, Shawzie looked at me with amazement and then asked to have Charles call her when he came home. She then suggested that I meet the President's daughter. I quickly replied that I couldn't possibly do that because of my hair. Her look told me that I was probably making a wise choice, and she left.

The driveway to my father's house was down a narrow hill that dead-ended at the house. As soon as Shawzie was gone, I ran to the window hoping to catch a glimpse of Margaret Truman. But what I saw was a driveway full of cars trying to figure out how to turn around in a very limited space.

When my father and Charles returned home, they were horrified that I wanted to charge the President's daughter twenty-five cents to go swimming. They immediately sent her a membership and told her that she would always be welcome at Unity. But she never came back. They thought it was because I was rude. I thought it was because the Secret Service drivers didn't like our driveway. When you are fourteen years old and you have just washed your hair and the President's daughter shows up wanting to go swimming, it's pretty hard to know how to respond.

That was then, and now Truman was no longer President. Perhaps I could make up for any ungraciousness I might have been guilty of by arranging a meeting between him and these Japanese religious leaders so that they might come together for a time of healing. I wrote, asking for an appointment. President Truman responded by very graciously inviting these gentlemen to visit him at the Truman Library in Independence. However, when Marc arrived at the Village with these men, they politely turned down Truman's invitation, and nothing we said could change their minds.

Once again I was in a very embarrassing situation. Since I had asked for the meeting, I had to be the one to call and cancel it. I can't remember what excuse I gave the President's secretary, but whatever it was, Mr. Truman, obviously, was not buying it. I know because I immediately received a letter from him. He wanted to make it very clear that he had very much wanted to meet these gentlemen, and it was *they* who refused the meeting. (It's good that I did not pursue a career in the diplomatic service!) Marc was extremely disappointed and so was I. I never got to meet President Truman, and Margaret still hasn't been swimming at Unity Village.

Now, a year or so later, I'm in Japan and these same men, representing different sects of Shinto, Buddhism, and other religions, are hosting a dinner in my honor at a beautiful Japanese restaurant in Tokyo. This was not for the others on the trip; it was just for me, arranged through the Unity connection. It was an evening I shall always remember. It was held in a private dining room, and I was the *only* woman guest present. If these gentlemen had wives, they were not included. While at Unity Village, these men wore dark suits and looked very much like businessmen, but in Japan they were dressed in colorful robes.

We were seated on mats placed around a very low table. Beautiful Japanese ladies attired in lovely kimonos were assigned to each person and, without in any way being intrusive, made it their responsibility to see that sake glasses were never empty, that course after course was served with the fluidity of a ballet ensemble.

As I looked around the room, I felt like Dorothy in *The Wizard of Oz* when she exclaimed, "Toto, I have a feeling we're not in Kansas anymore." These men spoke no English and I spoke no Japanese. They had, however, invited a young translator, who translated the toasts and short speeches for me as well as he could. Unfortunately, I couldn't understand his English much better than I could their Japanese, so I mostly had to guess at what was being said. Perhaps it was better that way, as I imagined wonderful poetic words which might have been dully prosaic had I actually been able to understand them.

Japan was the first stop on our world journey, and it was also the first time I had been in a country so far from home, and I had much to learn. One day I left our group in Tokyo to visit some Unity friends in Kyoto. I had their address, but it was written in English; with the naiveté of a truly inexperienced traveler, I thought this was all I needed to find my friends.

When I arrived in Kyoto, I eagerly hopped into a cab and gave the driver the paper with the written address. He nodded enthusiastically and away we went. I soon discovered that his English was limited to "Okay" and "No." My Japanese was even more limited. I knew only one word: *Sayonara.*

After much driving, I realized we were lost and that the driver didn't know any more than I did about where my Japanese friends lived. Finally, after some inspired sign language, I figured out that he was going to take me to a police station and leave me there. As I was contemplating my predicament, the cab was forced to slow to a snail's pace because of traffic and people. Looking in dismay at the sea of humanity that surrounded us, I happened to gaze upward and there in a window saw the familiar pictures of my grandfather and grandmother! You can imagine my relief to see their wonderful faces looking down at me. I jumped out of the cab, paid the driver, and ran up the staircase to my friends' apartment.

Although they were Japanese, they spoke fluent English. The woman explained that something had told her, just a few minutes before I arrived, to take the pictures of Charles and Myrtle Fillmore from the usual place she kept them and put them in the window!

Because of this experience and others, I truly believe that I was receiving divine protection on this trip. There were many times when, either through carelessness or ignorance, I could have had unfortunate things happen, but they didn't. Someone always appeared to help me when I needed it.

For instance, we stopped in Beirut to change planes. Beirut at that time was a beautiful city known as the Riviera of the Middle East. Nevertheless, then as now, you felt the tension and unrest. The Beirut airport was teeming with people of every nationality. Travel was complicated because you could not fly directly from Israel to an Arab country, and the use of passports and visas was a complex issue.

I was sitting quietly, waiting for our plane to leave, when I heard my name, in the midst of all the Arabic and French, being called over the loudspeaker system. The page was telling me to come to the airline information desk. Our plane was also being called so I had to hurry. When I finally found the desk, the man handed me my passport. A gentleman with an Arab headdress and long flowing robes had found it lying somewhere in the airport! I had no idea that I had lost it, and the airport official chastised me for being so careless and told me over and over again how fortunate I was that it had been picked up and returned to me by the man because passports were worth a great deal on the black market. The man refused any reward; he simply bowed, smiled, and quickly disappeared into the crowd.

I was shaken by the experience. Our next stops were Iran and Russia. We were in the middle of the Cold War; had I arrived in Russia without a passport and a visa, it would not have been a pleasant thing. But I didn't; an angel had once again come to my rescue. He probably didn't know he was an angel, but to me he was—or on the other hand perhaps he did know!

That long-ago journey introduced me to worlds so far removed from the one I had lived in up until that time; it was almost as if I had entered a different universe. In Hong Kong, I saw hundreds of refugees from communist China living in makeshift shacks and sampans, which are a kind of flat-bottomed rowboat. I saw hungry children who would fight one another for a bite of food. There was one particular experience I shall always remember.

We had hired a car and driver to take us around the city to do some filming. I had been warned not to give children money when they begged because it would only cause trouble. But this time we were parked in a quiet spot overlooking the sea. A little girl approached and held out her hand for some money for food. I looked all around me and could see no other children or any other people. She was so small and helpless that I could not resist handing her some American dollars. The minute I did, more children appeared, seemingly from nowhere. They surrounded the poor little girl, knocked her to the ground and started fighting with one another over the small amount of money I had given her. Another group of children started after us. The driver told us to get inside quickly and lock the door, which we did. He then backed the car around and sped away. I felt terrible. I wanted to go back and help the little girl; if I hadn't given her money, these children would not have turned into an angry mob. But the driver insisted that we keep going. He explained that there were hundreds of children in Hong Kong at that time who were hungry and desperate, and we would only cause more trouble if we returned. I have never forgotten that experience. To this very moment I can see as vividly as if it were yesterday that little girl sadly and quietly sitting on the ground as the other children fought with one another over the gift I had tried to give her.

From Hong Kong, we went to Vietnam. At the time we arrived in Saigon, the United States had not formally entered the war; nevertheless the city was already filled with American military personnel. When we interviewed the general in charge, he explained that American personnel were there only in an "advisory capacity." Saigon was a beautiful city populated by warm, friendly people. However, the sounds of gunfire in the distance left its populace anxious and fearful.

I was especially impressed by the dainty, lovely Vietnamese women. Their national dress, a tunic worn over flowing trousers, enhanced their small, graceful figures. It is certainly not surprising that many American servicemen brought these lovely women home as their wives.

One evening our group was invited to a party, hosted by President Ziem at the National Palace. The many-course dinner ended with President Ziem expressing deep appreciation for the help America was giving to his country. Sometime after our return home, President Ziem was killed in a coup, which many thought was encouraged by the United States. The people who dined with us that evening were dignitaries in President Ziem's government. I often wonder what happened to them after his death. To understand the intricacies of another country's politics is hardly possible, especially when it is difficult to fathom our own.

Looking back on that time in Saigon in the early sixties, I wonder if someone had given President Kennedy the slightest clue as to where our military presence, even in a so-called advisory capacity, would lead America, couldn't he have said, "Pack your bags, boys, and come home quick"? America was becoming involved in a civil conflict, and the French before us had proved a foreign power attempting to win a war on the mainland of Asia is like—as they say in Jamaica—trying to carry water in a straw basket.

From Vietnam, we traveled to Thailand: a beautiful, exotic land where I entered, for a moment, a place so fanciful that even my wildest childhood imaginings could not have invented it. Little girls who live on farms in Missouri try to keep some realistic possibility even in their fantasies! We discovered on our arrival in Bangkok that our group had been invited to have tea with the King and Queen of Thailand at their summer palace on the Gulf of Siam. However, before we could go, it would be necessary to be instructed in royal protocol. It seems that there are some important dos and don'ts when being entertained by royalty. First, you wear gloves and you never, *ever* touch the King or Queen. No shaking hands, no pats on the back, no hugs (they obviously were concerned about how some gauche Americans might greet the King and Queen); the King and Queen are considered holy and no mortal human must ever touch them. The protocol officer explained that it wasn't too far back in Thailand's history that the Queen's Royal Barge capsized, and she drowned. No one was allowed to rescue her since that would involve touching!

We also had to try to learn how to curtsy, which isn't all that easy, especially if you are a tall, awkward person and the Queen is petite! In addition, we were given a whole list of subjects we were not supposed to discuss when having tea. Politics was not to be mentioned. We were told not to be surprised when the servants began serving the tea, as they would be walking in a very unusual manner, half crouch and half crawl; it was also against protocol for any subject to stand above the King and Queen.

We took our list of dos and don'ts back to the hotel to study, and the next day we were driven to the palace. Everyone was nervous, for fear they might make some inexcusable faux pas. However, on arrival we were soon put at ease by Thailand's beautiful and charming Queen and the young, earnest King. We had been told that the King had studied in America and was a devotee of American jazz, so when my turn came to speak with him I asked him what American musician he especially admired. Without hesitation his face lit up and with enthusiasm he replied, "Elvis Presley." As I moved away from the King and walked out on the lovely terrace overlooking the Gulf of Siam, around me servants were gracefully serving tea in positions most of us would have found impossible to duplicate. I felt as if I had wandered into a performance of *The King and I*, staged in modern dress. However, imagining Yul Brynner and Deborah Kerr dancing to the line "You ain't nothing but a hound dog" was so incongruous that I started to laugh. It seems there are few places on Earth that American pop culture has not invaded.

In India, we were fortunate to meet Prime Minister

Nehru. He spent an hour or so graciously answering our questions. He was nearing the end of his life, but when he spoke of his country and what had been achieved and what he still hoped to achieve, he emanated a strong vitality that was enhanced by his keen intelligence.

After spending time with Prime Minister Nehru, the King and Queen of Thailand, and King Hussein of Jordan and listening as they spoke of their countries and talked of their hopes and aspirations for their people, it became clear that when power politics are set aside there was a similar desire in each of them to do the best they could for the people they served and the country they loved. We were not allowed to film our meetings on this trip with the leaders because we were with a group, so they graciously invited us to return at a later date to film one-on-one interviews. I was very much surprised and saddened to hear of Nehru's death a year or so after our trip. I had hoped to return to India to film an interview with him, and he had agreed to do it. When he died, his daughter Indira Gandhi volunteered to fill his position.

In Jordan, we met with King Hussein. He received us in a rather stark reception hall in his palace. It was very different from the quiet luxury and elegance we had experienced in Siam. Here, instead of tea brought by crouching servants, we were served Turkish coffee by men who looked as if they had just ridden in from the desert.

King Hussein reminded one of a shorter, younger Clark Gable. He was a handsome, intense young man who was sitting on a very uneasy throne. Already, he had survived several attempts on his life. He and his country were vulnerable to the constantly shifting sands of Middle East political and religious unrest. At the time of our visit, Jerusalem was a split city, with part in Jordan and part in Israel, and you could not travel from the Arab section into the city. As I write this today, some forty years have passed. King Hussein is now gone, but the winds of discontent in this troubled land are as alive today as they were then. The King during his long reign somehow managed to keep his country centered in its search for peace. His understanding of both the East and West made his contribution to easing potentially volatile situations invaluable.

King Hussein was given by destiny a difficult role to play in a drama that seems to find no ending. He courageously played his part with an integrity and strength that are not often seen on the world stage. He was kind enough to invite us back to Jordan and even offered to take care of our expenses while we were in his country, but unfortunately, I could not persuade Unity School to let me do the series "Mission for Understanding," and I could not find other financing. It was a great disappointment to me because I felt and still feel today that Unity can serve as a healing bridge by helping people understand different faiths, different cultures, and different ways of living. I think my grandfather also felt that Unity had a part to play on the world stage.

David Ben-Gurion, Israel's great elder statesman, also invited us to come to the Negev desert to interview him. Since we weren't allowed to go to Israel on this trip, I never had the pleasure of meeting Mr. Ben-Gurion. I was very impressed that he would invite us to bring our small film crew to his desert home, since he didn't have a clue as to who we were or what we were all about, other than what I had explained in my letter.

After Jordan, we went to Cairo, Egypt. Our meeting with President Nasser was cancelled because someone had tried to assassinate him on the day we arrived! He was understandably not in the mood for entertaining strangers. From Egypt, we flew to Iran. Again we failed. The Shah and his Queen were in the United States, so instead of tea with the royals we were taken on a tour of the royal jewels. The young cinematographer who was doing the filming for our *Daily Word* program, Reza Badiyi, was Iranian and Tehran was his home. His family welcomed us into their home, and I was impressed by their warmth and graciousness when I knew they would have much rather given their full attention to their wandering son.

The poetry and romance of ancient Persia were still being expressed through the creative artistry and ingenuity of the Iranian people. Those I met were devout Muslims whose faith was the guiding principle in their lives. However, there was also a strange energy in Tehran that made me uncomfortable. It was like coming into a room where people have been having a very serious discussion, but stop when you enter. It was as if what we were experiencing was far different from what was actually happening in their country.

But if Iran was mysterious, there was no mystery at all in our next stop—Russia. It was absolutely clear that what we were seeing and hearing was exactly what the communist government wanted us to see and hear. Russia and America at that time were in the middle of the Cold War, and our government guides were friendly but distant. We met no Russian diplomats or government officials, and our hosts were as chilly as the weather.

I returned to Russia in 1989, and it was like a different country. Gorbachev was then President, and under his leadership, based on *glasnost* and *perestroika*, the Cold War was rapidly melting. People were now allowed to invite us into their homes, they talked freely about their lives, and we were even asked by a family club to come to one of their meetings to tell them about Unity. It was wonderful to see how things had changed. I was deeply touched by the sincere warmth of these wonderful Russian people who opened their hearts and homes to us.

From Moscow, we flew to East Berlin. To enter West Berlin it was necessary for us to walk, carrying our bags, through a kind of no-man's-land, which separated the two sections, to "check-point Charlie," where our bags were examined before we could enter the western side. When we were cleared to enter, it was as if we had stepped from

winter into the vibrancy of spring. The citizens of West
Berlin freely went about their city, engaging in their daily
activities without fear. Stores, restaurants, and businesses
were operating with a positive energy that was very different from the melancholy one felt in the East. The wall
that separated the two communities was a grim reminder
of humankind's futile attempt to keep the human spirit
from expressing freely. I remember that grim rampart,
with broken glass on top and flowers at the bottom, where
people had been killed trying to escape. In one place in
the West, we filmed a church where only a bulletin board
was left. It said in German, "And yet we are all brothers."

Later President Kennedy would declare, to roars of
applause, "*Ich bin ein Berliner*—I am a citizen of Berlin."
President Reagan would call, "Mr. Gorbachev, tear down
this wall!" And finally we would all see the riveting news-
reels of people doing just that. Robert Frost wrote,
"Something there is that doesn't love a wall,"[10] and that
something is always stronger than any form of repression.
The Berlin Wall is no longer there; it gave way to the
indomitable spirit within us which refuses to be held
hostage to anything that endeavors to keep it from soar-
ing upwards.

I returned from that long-ago trip with so many
thoughts, impressions, and questions that it was difficult
to put it all into perspective. In just forty days, I had been
introduced to a whirlwind of different cultures, religions,
and philosophies; yet the individuals I met in my travels

expressed the same basic desires, needs, and hopes for their families, their countries, and themselves. We are not really that different. It became very clear to me that the spiritual dimension of life is as vital to most of the Earth's population as the material. The hunger of the human soul to know God is universal and has nothing to do with the color of our skin, the shape of our eyes, or the language of our worship. It doesn't matter whether we call ourselves Christians, Hindus, Muslims, Jews, or whatever. Our earnest desire to experience God is the same, only our paths are diverse.

In India, I felt God's presence as I stood before the Gandhi memorial, saw the flowers laid in the letters of his name, and listened to the chanting of the many Hindus who had gathered there to pray.

The Muslim call to prayer, which echoed through the ancient streets of Jerusalem, had a mystical vibration which so permeated the atmosphere that one's soul resonated with the power. "There is no God but Allah. There is no God but Allah." The sound of the Muezzin call from the minaret is one I will never forget.

In Bangkok, Thailand, I meditated at the foot of the Golden Buddha. This is one of the most sacred places of the Buddhist faith. When we entered the temple, I could feel the awe and reverence generated by the accumulated faith over centuries. I took off my shoes at the door, just as everyone else did, and when I walked up to the enormous golden statue of Buddha, I knelt like the others, worshipping and meditating with them. Our cinematographer took pictures for us to use for our television program.

When the film began to be shown on television, I got blindsided. I started to receive letters from people who were very unhappy with me—actual hate mail. Many wrote, asking how I could allow myself to kneel down to "idols." My staff and I were shocked, because none of us had seen it coming. I hadn't even thought about it in that way. I wasn't kneeling down to an idol. I was praying to the spirit of the One God, which is found wherever people worship, and I certainly felt God's spirit in that beautiful Buddhist temple. My staff and I wrote to the people who were offended and tried to express our feelings. I'm not sure they understood. They had not had the benefit of growing up with my family and the extended family of the Unity workers.

In Unity, the emphasis is always on inclusion, not exclusion. I remember a little verse by Edwin Markham that was a favorite of my Uncle Lowell's; I have heard him quote it many times:

> He drew a circle that shut me out—
> Heretic, rebel, a thing to flout.
> But Love and I had the wit to win:
> We drew a circle that took him in.[11]

I'm so glad that in Unity we have never drawn a circle to shut anyone out. That's not to say that we accept everything taught by every religion, not at all. It is only that we accept all faiths as reaching out to God and believe that any step taken to know God is valid. It is difficult for me to understand why some Christian sects wish to exclude any religion that does not believe as they believe. It seems a strange interpretation of the teaching of Jesus Christ, who constantly emphasizes the importance of love—unconditional, nonjudgmental love.

We live on a planet that is becoming increasingly interdependent. We can no longer separate ourselves into exclusive societies. Separation will not work in a world of instant communication, in a nuclear world, in a world of economic dependency, in a world where ecology is a universal responsibility.

For me, a Christian, to say to a Muslim, Jew, or any person following another faith that my way is the only way to God would be insulting and diminishing to the Loving Intelligence that created a beautifully diverse universe.

Our journey of faith is uniquely our own, to exclude anyone is not only foolish but impossible. The most profound message of this trip for me was the strong reminder that although I lived in a little place called Unity Village in the heart of America, I was also a part of a much larger universe. That was why the movie we made about the trip began with this verse:

Faith is a bridge, a shining span,
Rising strong and broad,

Linking heart with human heart
And human heart with God.

A theme of that movie was walls, because we saw so
many of them—in Hong Kong, Jerusalem, and the Wall in
Berlin. Yet, beyond all the walls, all the divisions that
seem to separate us, beyond the chaos that continually
erupts somewhere on our planet, beyond the pain we
inflict upon one another, beyond the seeming inequities
of life, there is always purpose and meaning. It is especially important to know this in the face of recent devel-
opments in the world. I was frightened, even awed, by the
wall in Berlin. It seemed as if it could never come down.
Yet it has, and in my lifetime.

I am not—and you are not—a little, frightened,
lonely, isolated life. On the contrary, we are a part of a
vibrant, diverse universe that would not be complete
without our individual consciousness. Each human soul
is an integral part of the evolutionary process. Every
thought we think, every choice we make affects the
whole. Each soul is equally precious to the Loving Intelligence that created all life.

# 7. Waking Up

My world journey introduced me to conditions that were different from any I had been exposed to. I felt as Buddha must have when he left his palace and saw pain and suffering for the first time. This experience led him to the Bodi Tree and enlightenment, while forty years later I am still in the process of trying to wake up.

One time when I was participating in a women's group, I expressed how shy I had been as a child and a teenager and that I still suffered stage fright sometimes when I had a speaking engagement. One of the ladies in the group asked how I could possibly feel that way when I had been taught such a liberating philosophy. I tried to explain to her that just because you are raised by enlightened people doesn't mean that you are automatically going to become enlightened yourself. Enlightenment comes when we are ready to receive it; it is not in the genes like blond hair and blue eyes are.

Another experience was also instrumental in moving me out of my happy dreamworld into the realization that there were things going on around me which I had failed to notice in my self-involved complacency.

Although Unity Village is located in the Midwest, in the forties and fifties during my growing-up years, the people in the little town of Lee's Summit and the surrounding areas, including Kansas City, were as southern in their attitudes about race as people in the deep South were. There were only a very few black families living in Lee's Summit, and those that were there bussed their children to a neighboring town to go to a segregated black school. Consequently, I did not have one African-American friend. In fact, I rarely saw any black people even in Kansas City, since they lived in one section of the city and the white people lived in another. In retrospect, I am amazed that I never questioned why this was true. I did not even ask why there were no people of color in our school. I am sad to say that I suppose it was the old adage: "Out of sight, out of mind."

There were black students who attended the summer Unity Training School sessions: they lived in the same motel area as the other students, but there was one cottage complex set aside to house them. Again I never questioned why they had their own cottage. I was living in a segregated society, and my awareness was nil.

This was all happening around me as I was growing up, getting married, and having children. However, one day either God, my unconscious, or some disgusted angel must have decided that it was time for me to become conscious of something besides my world and myself. This happened when an air force officer who knew my husband Stanley asked him if he could employ a young Micronesian man whom he had met during his tenure in the Pacific. He had brought the young man back to the United States with him, but now he was being transferred to another base and could not take him along.

At that time we were living on a farm next to Unity Village. We had a very busy household—two children plus my job in television and Stanley's real estate business—so we readily agreed to employ Show.

When he arrived, we discovered he was from the island of Palau, a part of the Micronesian Island chain in the West Pacific. Show was a lovely, shy young man in his early twenties and was a long, long way from home. I am sure our world seemed strange to him, but he never complained, and our whole family felt blessed by his presence.

However, he was not with us very long before we discovered complications that neither my husband nor I had anticipated. The first thing happened a few weeks after his arrival when Show said he needed to get his hair cut. I never thought of this as a problem and neither did Stanley. We would simply take him to a barber in Lee's Summit. Well, it *was* a problem. When Stanley took Show to the barbershop, the barber refused to cut his hair because he was "a person of color."

We could find no one in the area where we lived to cut this gentle young man's hair. We found that he had to go to the African-American section of Kansas City, not only whenever he wanted to get a haircut but whenever he wanted to go shopping, see a movie, eat out, or whatever. Show had never experienced this kind of discrimination before, and he began to get very depressed. Our farm was a long bus ride to Kansas City, plus he had no friends when he got there. Having grown up on a happy, peaceful island where everyone was equally loved and accepted, it was difficult for Show to understand the rejection he was experiencing because of the color of his skin.

Eventually, he had a friend from Palau come to visit. Fortunately, we were able to get his friend a job at Unity Village, but after a year or two, homesickness got the better of both of them and they decided to return to Palau.

I was angry that this kind of ignorant, prejudiced, racist behavior was being expressed in the place where I had spent my life by people I thought I knew. I felt great guilt that I was part of a culture which felt it was all right to treat fellow human beings in such disgraceful, disrespectful ways. It dawned on me that I had gone about my own life with no real awareness or concern about how people of color were constrained by all kinds of discrimination as they tried to go about their daily lives. I was ashamed of my insensitivity, my lack of awareness, and my blindness.

Soon after Show left, I was once again confronted by how deeply embedded prejudice lays in the human psyche. Because I was active with the People-to-People Program, I was asked to help entertain ambassadors from the new states of Africa who had been invited to Kansas

City to participate in a special program by this organization. I was very happy that I had been asked to be a part of this activity and volunteered to give a dinner party for the ambassadors of Ghana and Nigeria.

When they graciously accepted my invitation, I looked forward to a wonderful evening. But to my dismay, when I started calling friends to invite them to my party, they all seemed to have previous engagements! I was truly shocked. It was difficult to believe that my friends were just too busy to spend an evening with dignitaries who were representing their countries as ambassadors to America. It was even harder to believe that they were busy because my guests were black, but I was forced to this opinion.

When it became evident that I was going to have trouble getting any of those who I had assumed were intelligent, unprejudiced people—and my friends—to come to dinner, I had to prevail on a good friend in the television industry to help me, Don Davis.

Don was president of a local television station and was responsible for putting our *Daily Word* program on TV. I had met Don when he was managing a radio station that carried a weekly program called "Young Ideas," which I produced and moderated. He was a vibrant, intelligent man who had little patience with racial intolerance. He had become indignant at the fact that most Kansas City clubs were closed to his Jewish and black friends—so indignant that he formed a new club in the downtown area, which was open to anyone who chose to join.

When I went to Don for help in getting the right people to the party for the ambassadors, he immediately jumped into action and our party became a very special evening for everyone who was fortunate enough to be there. Our guest list included Don and his wife Harriet; a wonderful Jewish Rabbi and his wife; an African-American Kansas City councilman and his wife; a friend of mine who worked at Unity, Pauline Denniston, who was also one of Kansas City's best vocalists; and of course my kids, my husband, and my dad. It was a memorable evening, and I think the ambassadors enjoyed themselves. But I remained astounded that friends, whom I had thought I knew well, carried within them such an unreasonable bias.

Thanks to Martin Luther King, Jr., and the freedom marchers of the sixties, America finally began to wake up and the cruel practice of segregation began to dissolve. It did not come easily; it happened only because of the dauntless spirit of those who were willing to risk their lives rather than continue to exist under such appalling discriminatory conditions. We have the progress we see now only because of the courage of those who were brave enough to refuse to go to the back of the bus, to insist they could attend the same schools as their white counterparts, to sit in restaurants until they were served. They took non-violent steps of protest, and they carried their cases legally to the courts, the American way, and America did begin to awaken. Schools were integrated, doors were opened, and no longer could any American be legally discriminated against. Young people today have never seen a restroom or drinking fountain in America marked "White Only."

In Unity, it was through the courageous insistence of Johnnie Colemon, who in 1955 was in Unity's ministerial training program, that Unity School finally transcended the morass of cultural bias which prevailed at that time and became integrated. Before Johnnie raised her voice in protest, people of color who came to study at the Village had to commute daily to and from Kansas City, since they were not allowed to live on grounds.

Today it is difficult to believe that Unity would participate in such blatant discrimination. The only excuse I can find, and a sorry excuse it is, is that Unity had never before become involved in social issues, and the School was simply following the culture of the community of which it was a part.

Johnnie Colemon let her voice be heard, and by so doing, she made an important contribution to Unity and its future. She is living proof that if you stand on principle and move forward with faith, there is no mountain that cannot be moved.

Johnnie became one of Unity's most successful graduates. She founded the Christ Universal Temple in Chicago, a church of some 15,000 members that serves people around the globe. Although her church is not formally affiliated with Unity, Johnnie does return to the Village occasionally to speak and participate in special programs.

It is my strong belief that Unity and the whole New Thought movement need to become more involved in social issues. Bad things are allowed to happen when good people remain silent and detached. If we are to remain relevant in a changing world, we must let our voices be heard.

Probably the person who was most responsible for raising Unity's social consciousness was David Williamson who, when Johnnie Colemon protested, led the ministerial candidates to rally around and support her. David grew up in Unity and became a Unity minister who served in several churches, notably in Detroit with a mostly black congregation, for many years. In the 1960s, he had come to Unity School to become director of the Ministerial Education Program.

David was always very concerned about the discrimination black Americans had experienced in the past, and he made it his mission while at the School to assure African-Americans that Unity Village welcomed their presence. He instituted sensitivity training for Unity executives and employees and made sure that there would be black teachers and counselors on staff.[12]

Dave Williamson was a gentle, caring soul who spent his entire life helping others to embrace their spiritual kinship. His contribution to the Unity movement was critical to its growth and unfoldment, and he will always be remembered with love and deep appreciation for all he gave to the human family.

To say that there is no more racism in our country is, of course, not true. Changing minds and hearts that have been immersed in generations of fearful, bogus, unrealistic thinking does not happen quickly; but slowly and surely it *is* happening. Why people should be discriminated against because of the color of their skin, their sex, or their religion is an enigma. That we have done this to one another is a tragic commentary on how slow humankind is in awakening to the realization of the divinity of each human soul.

Living now in Jamaica, I am in the minority group. However, even here in a predominantly black country, there is concern that some beautiful, young Jamaican girls are using harsh bleaching creams because they feel they would be more attractive if their skin were lighter. These lovely black women endanger themselves because somewhere, at some time, someone made them feel white is better. This kind of erroneous thinking must be eliminated from human consciousness if we are to move forward into "a new heaven and a new earth" (Rev. 21:1).

How do we eliminate it? By teaching our children that they are perfect just as they are and that the color of our skin, our sex, or our word for God has no bearing on their value as human beings. Every life is equally important to the Loving Intelligence that created all of us.

# 8. Questions and Revelations

I grew up believing in a loving God. In fact, one of the basic premises of Unity's philosophy is "There is but one presence and one power in the universe, God the good, omnipotent." However, if this is true, how do we explain places where starving children roam the streets? Places where religion and ethnic hatred are passed from generation to generation like some sacrosanct torch that must never be extinguished? Places where just the color of your skin, your genealogy, or your sex can engender hostility, fear, and subjugation? How do you reconcile a loving, omnipresent Intelligence with the fact that so many of the world's people are living in such unmitigated misery?

The religions of the world have a variety of explanations for why there is so much disparity in the human condition. Most of us subscribe to the theology that we are born into or the one we have chosen along the way. And then, of course, there are those who feel any religious answer is too abstract, too improbable, and believe, instead, in a random universe where it is all just a roll of the dice.

Unity's message—its answer—is that beyond the inequalities, beyond the walls (the divisions that separate the seeming haves and the havenots), beyond the chaos and the pain, beyond the surface turmoil, there is a divine intention that gives meaning to it all. If our vision could reach past the struggles, the strivings, the manipulations, we would find we are not just a little, lonely life; instead, we are one with all life. Although the energy of creation is constantly moving and changing, there is an underlying, orderly, evolutionary process evolving and what appears to be chaos is really transformation.

In Genesis, we are told that humans were made in the image and likeness of God and were given dominion over the Earth. If we believe this to be true, then the Earth we see today must have been created by *us*. If we want to have a different world, then we must begin using our creative power in ways that will heal and lift our planet instead of continually repeating the same destructive patterns.

During my years in Unity, I met many people who spoke of life-changing spiritual experiences. Some said they heard God's voice clearly speaking to them. Others felt the presence of Jesus. Still others described revelations that went beyond the ordinary. Of course, my grandfather was sure that he was guided by Spirit (God) in every way. Although I had seen the transforming power of faith, not only in my own family but also in the lives of so many others, I still felt I needed to have my own God-experience to truly understand my personal relationship with our Creator.

When I lived at Unity Farm, I loved to take long walks through the grounds. My favorite walk was around what we called "the loop." The loop was a road that started at the old greenhouse; proceeded down a hill past the amphitheater, the apartment houses, and the swimming pool; circled through a lovely wooded area; continued up another hill past my Uncle Lowell's home and the motels; and ended back at the greenhouse. I could not count the number of times I have walked the loop; even today, when I am back home, my children always ask me if I want to drive around the loop before we leave the Village. I realize that walk was as integral to their young lives as it was to mine.

There is one place, just after you leave the Clubhouse and enter the woods, where another road juts off the loop and leads to the picnic grounds. I would take this path if I wanted to stop for a while and meditate. At one time there were cabins in the woods nearby, which people could use for holidays; two were eventually made into small homes for Unity workers. All but one are gone now. The one that remains, named "Harmony House," was my son's home when he was first married but that was years after the time I was on my search for a God-experience. At the time I am speaking of, my son was still a little boy. Few people came to this part of the Village during the week, and with its peaceful, natural beauty it was a good place to meditate. The picnic area had several tall walnut trees, which shaded picnickers on hot summer days. When I was a little girl, in the fall Helen and I would gather the nuts that had fallen on the ground; then on cold winter nights, we

would shell them before the fireplace. Years later I still
loved this special place; it seemed the ideal spot for me to
try to communicate with God. So every day I made my pil-
grimage to these grounds. I found a place to sit on a low
wall that encircled a lovely, natural-stone oven that my dad
had built for people to roast hot dogs and marshmallows.

I would close my eyes and try to enter a meditative
state, but days passed and I heard no voice, I felt no presence, and—although I enjoyed the peace and quiet—no
revelation came to me. On the day I had decided I would
have to give up my search and continue to rely instead on
other people's revelations, I became aware of a gentle
breeze caressing my cheek. I opened my eyes and became
conscious of the beauty surrounding me. As I looked to
the woods, I saw the soft tones of autumn beginning to
form on the trees. It was as if an artist's brush were deli-
cately changing the green leaves of summer into the more
vivid reds and yellows of fall. The small animals of the
woods were busy gathering provisions for the coming winter. Everywhere I looked I saw the harmonious flow of
nature as summer was slowly changing into autumn.

As I marveled at the orderly progression of seasons,
something inside of me asked: "Don't you know that this
same orderly process is at work in you? There are changing seasons in human life just as in nature." It was as if
some wiser, higher me were speaking to the unsure,
searching me. "How can you doubt that I exist when you
are a part of this amazing universe? Do you think a con-

stantly changing cosmos has no order or design, that everything just happens, that there is no intelligence behind the multifarious expressions of existence? Of course, you don't believe that.

"Well then, if all life came from a loving creative intelligence, would that intelligence remove itself from the wonder it created? Would a loving father or mother give birth to a baby and then say, 'I brought you into the world and now you are on your own; I'm out of here'? If they did, they would be jailed for child abandonment! So why would a loving Creator abandon its creation?

"There is no reason to search for Me when I am a part of you. I am closer than your heartbeat, nearer than your breathing. I am in every experience, in every person; I am in those you love most and in those who have caused you pain and despair. I am always here, guiding you, loving you. But to feel My presence, to hear My Truth, you must quiet your busy thoughts, still your anxious mind, and let My peace enfold you—My love embrace you. It is in the silence that you hear Me. It is when the mind is still that the soul listens."

I shall never forget that experience. When the world is too much with me, in my mind I retreat to that lovely place where I first became aware that if I listen, if I really listen, God's loving intelligence is always there with me, ready to guide and direct my way.

"Be still, and know that I am God!" (Ps. 46:10)

# 9. For Everything a Season

Just as there are changing cycles in nature, there is an orderly change of seasons in our individual life. Life is a continuous process of growth and change.

We accept the changing cycles in nature; even look forward to them. It gives us reassurance that there is harmony in the universe, and even when we experience droughts or hurricanes, we know that eventually the rains will come or the winds will cease and the seas will calm. But in our lives, if changes arise unexpectedly we are apt to become anxious and fearful.

Many of the most wonderful changes in nature would seem terribly disturbing to the creature experiencing them if that creature thought as we do. For instance, imagine the hermit crab when he feels the shell that protects him growing tighter and tighter and knows he is growing too big for it. We would be terrified at the idea of going out without a shell into a world always ready to eat us and trusting to find another in time.

Or imagine the tadpole as it finds its tail gradually fading away and funny-looking legs beginning to sprout from its body. We would fear that our power to swim would be destroyed. We would not hunt food or escape our enemies, not to mention would be turning into a freak.

Or imagine the larva of the monarch butterfly when its muscles grow heavy and it feels the urge to build a case that potentially could be its own coffin. What gives it the courage to seal itself into that coffin and compose itself for apparent death? Surely it cannot foresee the exquisite winged creature it will become when it splits the coffin and flies away.

The crab, the tadpole, and the infant butterfly are not troubled by anxious emotions or negative thoughts because they live by the laws of nature and instinctively know that what is happening to them is the way it is supposed to happen.

We, on the other hand, are reasoning beings and have been given the gift of free will. We use our intelligent, reasoning powers to question, to doubt, and to fear the unknown. So often the poets express our dilemmas, and the Robert Burns poem "To a Mouse" is about this very problem of ours, as opposed to the creatures of nature. The poet, who was also a farmer, tells of turning up the nest of a field mouse with his plow. The mouse is not hurt and Burns apologizes as it scuttles away. But then he says to the mouse:

> Still thou art blest compared wi' me!
> The present only toucheth thee:
> But och! I backward cast my e'e

On prospects, drear!
An' forward though I canna see,
I guess an' fear![13]

Life is energy, movement, change. From the moment
we arrive on Earth, we are moving forward on our journey. The baby grows into the child. The child becomes the
adolescent. The adolescent moves into adulthood. And so
it goes until the soul once again leaves the body and goes
forth into another dimension of living. "For everything
there is a season, and a time for every matter under
heaven" (Eccl. 3:1).

The first season of my life began as it does for everyone, with my birth. For me, my birth was followed by a
happy, carefree childhood spent in a magical kingdom
where everything was good and beautiful. But childhood
cannot last forever, and my mother's death when I was in
my early teens made me realize that there is nothing we
can do to hold back the changing tides. Things happen
that we never dreamed could happen. In the so-called
"blink of an eye," circumstances can turn blissful naiveté
into the pain of loss.

My mother's death was soon followed by the bombing of Pearl Harbor: the safe, secure world of my childhood was over. All through my high school and first two
years of college, World War II was the focus of everyone's
thoughts and energies. Many of the boys with whom I
went to high school enlisted as soon as they were old

enough to be accepted. Some were killed; many were injured. My best friend's brother lost a leg. A lifeguard that I had dated became a prisoner of war.

In my college dorm, some nights we would be awakened by the screams of a fellow student who had received a call telling of the death of a brother, a fiancé, a friend. It was sad and frightening to hear those cries in the night. I'm sure others were praying, as I did, that no nocturnal call would come to our door.

I talked my dad into letting me go for a weekend visit with my piano-playing boyfriend before he went away to war. He agreed only if I would take our dear housekeeper Helen with me as my chaperone. Wesley was his name, and he was finishing his basic training at an army camp in Arkansas. The train from Kansas City to Little Rock was packed with soldiers. I remember thinking as I looked at those fresh young faces that soon they would be on troop ships traveling to some far-away battleground that they probably had not even heard of until the war began.

My friend was lucky. Because of his ability to play the piano, he was assigned to assist an army chaplain in the European theater; consequently, he was spared active combat duty. When he returned home after the war, the world had changed and so had we and our young love became a sweet memory. However, I always remember Wesley with great fondness. He brought music into my life. One of the best parts of my high school years was going with him to listen to the great bands that came to Kansas City—very different from today's hip-hop and rap! It was a wonderful era for music, and I'm so grateful that Wesley shared with me his appreciation and knowledge of the fine musical artists of that time; he opened a window to a world I might not have known.

But when one season ends and another begins, we have to move on. It was time for me to grow up.

My journey into adulthood began with my marriage at the age of twenty-one, followed a year later by the birth of my son Rick, and twenty-two months after that the birth of my daughter Rosalind.

Learning to be a wife and mother was, for me, pure on-the-job training. Nothing in my past experience prepared me for marriage or parenthood. Looking back at that time, I realize my children and I really grew up together and in many ways they progressed much faster than their mother.

In the first years of my children's lives, my attention was wholly focused on their care. In the early fifties, most women were stay-at-home moms, cheerfully giving up the jobs they had so successfully filled during World War II. Few women ventured into the business world unless it was absolutely necessary. This, however, was not how I was raised.

As I've written earlier, my grandmother worked with her husband in creating Unity, and she was actively involved in the work until she made her transition. She was so far from being a traditional housewife that she had her house at Unity Farm built without a kitchen! It was women who primarily sustained the infrastructure of Unity by working with true dedication in the many departments of Unity School. It was also the women, in the beginning of the Unity ministry, who courageously pioneered Unity centers across America.

Although I loved being at home with my children, I knew that when they reached school age I would return to Unity, hopefully, to work in broadcasting. The work at Unity was not an unknown land to me. Throughout my adolescence, I always had a summer job either at Unity Farm or at Unity headquarters, which was at that time at 917 Tracy in Kansas City, Missouri.

When I was about thirteen, I spent a few hours each day in what was called the Unity Training School for ministers and licensed teachers. It was housed in a building that was built for Silent Unity, but because of the depression of the thirties and then World War II, Silent Unity was not able to move to the Village until the early fifties. In the meantime, this building was used for summer classes. One section was also made into dormitory rooms for the people who came to study. My job was to sort mail, give people their keys, and do any other "gofer" type job that came along.

The Training School was managed by Dr. Leroy Dale. I have no idea what he was a doctor of, although I think it might have been chiropractic because when my dad wasn't feeling well Dr. Dale would come and massage his back and recite affirmations. Dr. Dale was an unforgettable character. Dogs and women loved him. He was a big, rather rough-looking man with a heart of gold and a voice louder than God's. The students had their meals at the Unity Inn, and before every meal, Dr. Dale would give a blessing that consisted of shouting a series of affirmations that blessed everything—from the food to whatever he considered important at the moment. At that time Unity Inn was strictly vegetarian, featuring delicacies like barbecued vegeburgers, chickette stew, and the best fudge sundae pie you ever ate. I recall the sight of Dr. Dale leading a group at "fast-march" around the quadrangle walk at Unity, breathing through one nostril at a time (by stopping the other with a finger) and chanting loudly, "I am a son of the living God, I am, I am, I am!"

Visitors often came to eat at the Inn. I used to think those who had just stopped for a quiet meal and caught Dr. Dale's performance must have wondered if they had wandered into some sort of mental institution!

Unity used to have many more "characters" than it has today—perhaps because it tolerated them better. And you couldn't help liking Dr. Dale. Nothing seemed to faze him. His spirit was always positive, and he had that masculine magnetism I mentioned that attracted women and dogs. In fact, I had a dog named Sheba who fell in love with Dr. Dale. She would wait outside the Training School office until we had finished for the day; then, ignoring me, she would happily follow him and off they would go together. I would be left standing by myself, calling, "Come back, little Sheba!" like the character in the William Inge play. It is a humbling experience to have your own dog forsake you for another.

My second job was being the summer daytime switchboard operator for Unity Village. I especially liked this job because the switchboard was on the first floor of the Unity Tower and my dad had a desk there, as did two or three other people. My father's studio was on the seventh floor of the Tower, but he met people and did his correspondence downstairs. I also liked operating the switchboard because I could talk to people. Finally, the Tower was a busy place with lots of activity that kept things from getting dull—or as teenagers would say "boring."

Each morning the postman from Lee's Summit would deliver the mail for the Village to this office. His name was Mr. Metheny, and his son Dave would help him carry in the mailbags. Dave was a good-looking boy who attended the same high school I did. He also played the trumpet in the Unity Band. This was a famous Unity institution, which for years was directed by the head of Unity's Radio Department, Dr. Carl Frangkiser, who was the bandleader of the Ringling Brothers Circus for many years. Every Sunday night during the summer, the Unity Band played a concert in the outdoor amphitheater, and hundreds of people from all the surrounding counties came to Unity Village to hear them.

When Dave grew up, married, and had a family, his two sons, Mike and Pat, became accomplished musicians, and they, too, played in the Sunday concerts. Pat Metheny is now a multiple Grammy Award winner and one of the finest jazz guitarists in the world. Early in his career, he wrote and recorded a song called "Unity Village." Dave and his wife Lois still live in the Lee's Summit area and are two of my dearest friends.

One summer my brother and I both worked at the Unity offices in Kansas City, about twenty miles from Unity Farm. I was assigned to the bindery. At that time there was no air-conditioning, and it was some hot job! The bindery prepared the magazines for mailing. First, brown paper wrappings were put around each magazine, followed by address labels, which were stamped on each periodical. This was done on an assembly line. As the magazines came down a moving belt, each person on the line had a specific task to perform. If you goofed, it broke the rhythm of the whole line. We worked from eight until five with a half-hour break for lunch. It was a long, hot summer, and for the first time I found myself looking forward to getting back to school.

After I left college, I worked a year in Silent Unity. Before you could become a Silent Unity letter writer, you were required to spend at least six weeks in the card and letter files, filing all the correspondence that came to Silent Unity. In truth, I can't remember whether it was six weeks that seemed like six months, or whether it really was six months. Whatever—the monotony was so dulling that at times I found myself longing for the bindery.

After your tenure of working with the card and letter files, you moved into Junior Letter Writers. Silent Unity was housed on the third floor of the Tracy Building. The first floor consisted of a reception area, a couple of private offices, the Accounting Department, the Field Department, and Mail Opening. The second floor housed the Letter Writers who took care of magazine subscriptions and business mail, plus their file systems. If you wrote about magazines and asked for prayers in the same letter, you were answered by two sets of letter writers, since Silent Unity was entirely separate.

The third floor held that world apart, which was Silent Unity. There were only two private offices. One was for the director of Silent Unity, who at that time was a lovely lady named May Rowland. The other was a very small enclosed space for the editor of *Daily Word* magazine—Martha Smock. One large room held the more trained and experienced Senior Letter Writers on one side and Junior Letter Writers on the other. Each desk was equipped with a typewriter—manual, of course, at that time—and you had to be able to type forty words a minute to become a letter writer.

I soon learned that the fundamental intent of Silent Unity was prayer and then more prayer. Each morning, our day began at 8 o'clock in the small assembly hall, which was separated from the Letter Writers' room by a short hallway. Everyone who worked in Silent Unity gathered in this room to begin the day with the reading of the *Daily Word*, followed by a time of meditation and prayer. At 8:30 we went to our respective desks and answered mail until 11 a.m., when we returned to the Prayer Room for the Healing Meeting. Every person who called or wrote to Silent Unity had his or her name placed in a prayer box in what was called the "holy room." These names were kept there and prayed with for thirty days or more.

Prayer never stopped; each worker also had an individual half-hour prayer time in the holy room. When your prayer time there was complete, you announced the next person's turn by placing on his or her desk a special picture of Jesus.

But a person calling for prayers didn't even have to wait for the name to get in the box; the Silent Unity Phone Room was also located on the third floor where trained prayer ministers took phone calls "twenty-four seven," as they say now. There was never a time when one or more persons were not praying in the Phone Room. It is from the Phone Room, first at 917 Tracy and now in the Silent Unity Building at Unity Village, that the symbolic light shines that is never put out. These never-ending prayers have continued now for over 110 years.

After the 11 o'clock Healing Meeting, we went to lunch at the Unity Inn, which was in another building. When we returned from lunch, we had a short prayer time at our desks before we began our afternoon work schedule. At 2:30 p.m. we all went to another meeting in the assembly room. This meeting consisted of either a talk about the purpose of Unity or a discussion about how to answer various prayer requests. Everything written to Silent Unity was absolutely confidential so no names were ever mentioned, only the type of response Silent Unity would make to different prayer requests.

In between all these prayer times, we also had letter-writing classes and pamphlet classes. Each correspondent not only received a special letter but also was sent a small pamphlet designed for his or her particular prayer request. Most letters and calls were for healing, prosperity, or human relationships, but whatever the request, it received a pamphlet and a prayer.

Every single letter and call was handled personally by a dedicated Silent Unity worker, and prayer was a way of life in the other departments of Unity as well. The letters were prayed over in Mail Opening even before they were opened, in the various daily Silent Unity meetings, and again after they were sealed and sent to the Mailing Department. Each bag of mail was again prayed over before it went off in the truck to the Post Office. I remember when I worked in the bindery we prayed over the magazines at the close of every day before they were sent to be mailed. I wonder if the people who received mail from Unity had any idea how much prayer had blessed it on its way to them.

Although prayer was the keynote of the Silent Unity

work, it was also a very happy, friendly work environ-ment. Because our desks were right next to one another, we all grew to know each other very well. It was like being a part of a large family where everyone worked together for a common goal.

During my tenure in Silent Unity, the ministerial students also worked in Silent Unity in the afternoons. The Ministerial Training School at that time was headed by James Dillet Freeman. He had been a protégé of Myrtle Fillmore, who first met him when he was a young boy. After graduating from the University of Missouri, he came to work for Unity. Jim, as his friends know him, has been extremely important in the unfoldment of Unity's mission in our world. Not only is he Unity's poet laureate, but he is also the author of many books, and after May Rowland's retirement, he became director of Silent Unity and even-tually first vice president of Unity. Even today, at ninety-something, Jim is still featured in *Unity Magazine* and *Daily Word*.[14]

But back in the time I was working at Silent Unity, Jim was about the same age as his students and was regarded by the women who worked in Silent Unity as the young, often-misunderstood poet who must be mothered and protected from a sometimes harsh world. To me, Jim became something like an older brother, who enjoyed teasing me, and to this day, our friendship remains pretty much the same. I always tell him that he took all the romance out of the Moon for me after I found out that

two astronauts, on different trips, had taken his writings
and placed them there. One was Buzz Aldrin and the
other was James Irwin, who later visited Unity Village and
wore his space suit for a talk. How can the Moon hold any
mystery for me? I look up at it and, instead of thinking of
the wonder of men actually traveling there, I think
instead: Not only has Jim been baiting me since I was a little kid here on Earth, now he's on the Moon too. There's
no escape! (At least, that's what I tell him but, in truth, I
am in awe of that fact!)

Two of Jim's pupils in the ministerial school at that
time were Eric Butterworth and Ralph Rhea. They had
entered the school after the War—that's how people of
my generation tend to refer to World War II. Little did
I know then that some twenty years later Ralph would be
my husband.

Ralph and Eric were quite different. Eric was a serious, shy person whom the girls liked to kid because he
blushed so easily. Ralph was just the opposite; he kept
everyone laughing, and practical jokes were his middle
name. In fact, one almost got him fired. The Midwest was
experiencing a severe drought and Silent Unity had been
praying daily for rain. Ralph and a friend decided those
prayers should not go unanswered. They went up on the
roof and hooked up hoses. When the group began praying for rain, they sprayed water down on the window-
panes that encircled one side of the "healing room."

Everyone thought it was a great prank—except the

prayer leaders. There were some discussions among them as to whether Ralph and his friend should remain working at Unity, since they did not seem to understand the sacrosanctity of prayer. Personally, I have always wondered why people seem to deny God a sense of humor, when we all have one born in us. Fortunately, they decided that "boys will be boys," and Ralph went on to become one of Unity's best ministers. Eric Butterworth overcame his shyness and became not only one of the movement's finest ministers but also the author of some of its most popular and influential books.[15] I'm sure the discipline and spiritual nurturing these young men received while working and studying in Silent Unity became great assets in their future ministries. In fact, looking back on the people who worked in Silent Unity as part of their ministerial training, it becomes evident that a great many of them went on to become some of the most dedicated, successful ministers in the history of the ministerial program.

I worked in Silent Unity Letter Writing for only a few months, until I became secretary to Martha Smock, then editor of *Daily Word*. It's difficult to believe, at this point and time in my life, that anyone would let me be his or her secretary; my skills must have been better at twenty, but I still doubt that they were very good. My training and desires had always been focused on radio, and typing—whether of letters or copy—was not one of my finer accomplishments. However, working with

Martha was a joy. She was a beautiful person with a good sense of humor, which I'm sure she needed with me as her assistant! She also knew that my time with her would be brief, as I was leaving to get married in a few months.

When I worked for Martha, she was pregnant with her first child. She was one of those women who grew more beautiful each day her pregnancy progressed. She was a lovely looking person to begin with, but in her pregnancy her face took on a Madonnalike quality—the Madonna of the Old Masters, not the singer—as if some soft light had been turned on inside her.

Martha was a fine writer and a fine editor. Under her guidance, *Daily Word* experienced a great increase in subscribers. She intuitively seemed to know what lessons and articles would be most helpful to the *Daily Word* readers. Martha herself has authored some of Unity's most beautiful writings. If you have never read her book *Meet It With Faith*,[16] I urge you to do so.

Martha and I remained close friends throughout her lifetime. In fact, Martha, Jim, and—of course—Ralph have been such an integral part of my journey that I cannot imagine what my life would have been without them.

The three people who have been my most important mentors in Unity were women: Martha Smock, Sue Sikking, and Mary Kupferle. These three women were very different in their personalities, but they also had many qualities that were similar. All three had a great sense of humor, and each of them was blessed with remarkable spiritual insight. If you read their books, you won't find intellectual or metaphysical musings. Instead, you will discover basic Truth expressed by women who were inspired by Spirit to express their faith in ways that give their readers faith and hope. Martha and Sue are no longer with us, but Mary is still writing. The last time I spoke to her on the phone, she was excited about a group of children's stories she was about to have published.[17] Another Unity minister, Gwen Norment, who now lives in Bellingham, Washington, has been a very special friend since we first met in the early sixties. Gwen and I are the same age, and we have shared a kinship of spirit that has been a precious part of my life. She is a beautiful, caring soul whose friendship has enriched my life in so many ways. I'm deeply grateful that I have known these women. Each of them contributed so much to the Unity movement, and I'm sure thousands of lives have been inspired by their wisdom and inspiration. Personally, they were friends who were there for me when I needed a friend. Without their love and support, my life choices might have been different.

Sue and Mary both invited me to be a part of their ministries when I was very much in need of a place to go. There was a gap of fifteen years between the two invitations, but each came at a significant turning point in my life. It was as if the intuitive Spirit within these two connected with my Spirit, and it became apparent that it was time for some human angels to appear. If you are thinking that sounds a little flaky, think about your own life. I'll wager you will discover that someone appeared to point the way when you were unsure of your path.

Of course, there are times when we are going through a difficult experience and we can find no evidence of any kind of angel, guardian, or human. If we do have any, they seem to be out to lunch—permanently. But from my own experience, I have complete faith that there is a divine messenger in all our experiences, even those which seem most painful and difficult.

I have been especially aware of protection and help when I traveled. There is always someone who says: "Let me show you the way. Let me help you. Let me share with you." It never ceases to amaze me how these kind, wonderful strangers can appear in such diverse and unlikely surroundings—in a crowded airport or on an almost deserted ferry station on a tiny island in the Atlantic Ocean. One time my angel was a pit boss in a gambling casino in Las Vegas—but that's another story!

Silent Unity is the very heart of the Unity movement, and each person who has worked there has contributed to the prayer consciousness that now reaches around the world. Today *Daily Word* is sent to 140 countries and printed in seven languages. Over a million people are reading the same daily message, constituting a powerful prayer network that reaches around our globe.

I shall never forget one afternoon, not too long ago, when I was sitting in my office at Unity Village. A tour guide tapped at my door to invite me to meet a special visitor. The visitor was a lovely French Polynesian woman who had traveled to Unity Village from a small island in the South Pacific that was located a thousand miles from Tahiti. She had flown halfway around the world to thank Silent Unity for their prayers for her husband, who had recovered from a serious heart attack. She said she felt she had to come personally to express her appreciation because she was so grateful that her husband was now well.

I am always in awe of how Unity has found its way into so many far-away places. However, I should not be surprised, because the energy of united prayer knows no boundaries.

I'm deeply grateful for my time in Silent Unity. Even though I never worked there after leaving to be married, when I returned to Unity School to work in radio and television, I always tried not to miss the 11 o'clock Healing Meeting.

Another person who played a vital role in the evolution of Unity was a man named Otto Arni. I first met Otto when he was working in the Accounting Department at 917 Tracy. Otto came to work for Unity when he was just out of high school. He left to serve in the navy during World War II, but after the war he immediately returned to Unity. Eventually Otto moved from Accounting to become my father's right-hand man in the development of Unity Village. Otto has served Unity in many different capacities including treasurer of the Board of Directors.

Working at Unity School was never just a job for the people who were instrumental in its growth and unfoldment. I know that Martha, Jim, and Otto were as passionate about Unity as the Fillmores. It was their life, and all of them gave their time, their energy, their love to helping the dream become reality.

In my mind's eye, I can still see the excitement in Martha's eyes as she read a letter from a *Daily Word* reader who had written to express thanks. Otto, now retired, still drives each day through the Village, looking, I'll wager, with eyes of love at all he helped create.

Three kids, Martha, Jim, and Otto, walked through the doors of 917 Tracy to begin what they thought would be their first job. Little did they know that they were about to fall in love with an idea that would not only change their lives, but through their creative spirit and dedication would bless the lives of thousands upon thousands of people not only on this planet but also in outer space. Remember, each time you gaze at the Moon James Dillet Freeman's "Prayer for Protection" is shining down upon you:

> The light of God surrounds you;
> The love of God enfolds you;
> The power of God protects you;
> The presence of God watches
>     over you.
> Wherever you are, God is.

# 10. The *Daily Word* on TV

As I look back on my life, I realize how many serendipitous meetings brought forth amazing results. As I mentioned previously, I met Don Davis when I approached him with my idea about having a weekly radio program for young people on his station. He accepted the program, and it aired every Saturday afternoon. A year or so after I met Don, he left the radio station to become the manager of one of the local network television stations in Kansas City. The time was the mid-fifties, and television was an exciting new medium.

Although Don did not attend a Unity church, he had become interested in the Unity philosophy. One day he called me at home to tell me that he had a great idea, and he wanted me to arrange a meeting with "the powers that be" at Unity School. His idea was to put *Daily Word* magazine on television. He explained he would provide free time for a daily five-minute program, and he wanted me to be the presenter.

I was flabbergasted. I had never thought of being on television, and the prospect of sitting in front of cameras talking made me extremely anxious. However, everyone else thought it was a wonderful opportunity for Unity; and, of course, I could do it.

I had always hoped that someday I could be a part of Unity radio outreach, but television was a whole different ball game. I then remembered my grandfather's prediction that someday I would be in films.

In the mid-fifties, television was still such a new experience that people were willing to look at almost anything that moved on that little screen in their living rooms, and I think this was my saving grace.

"The *Daily Word*" was broadcast live, each Monday through Friday morning at 10:55. Its five-minute segment came right after "Romper Room" and just before "Whizzo the Clown." This meant that while I was reading and expounding on the *Daily Word* lesson, one group of kids was being ushered out of the studio as another group was ushered in. It made for some rather interesting programming at times.

After we were on the air for about a year, Don decided we should go to film—this was before videotape—and syndicate the program across America. On November 4, 1957, we began syndication with twenty-three stations, and eventually we were in eighty-seven cities, which included all the major markets. The stations gave us free time, and we provided the *Daily Word* feature.

The filming was done by a small company in Kansas City called Horizon Productions, owned and operated by Bill Longmoor and Bob Nelson. Tragically, Bill Longmoor, years later, was killed in the collapse of the walkway in Kansas City's Hyatt Hotel. The photographer on the show was Tony Latona, who later worked for Unity School. Henry Effertz, locally well-known, was the announcer; and Reza Badiyi, who would later accompany me on my media trip abroad, was director.

In a foreshadowing of what was to come with "The Word," we once had actor John Payne, best known for the film *Miracle on 34th Street*, and Mala Powers, Roxanne to Jose Ferrer's *Cyrano de Bergerac*, as guests on the program.

The Publicity Department at Unity School handled the mechanics of the preparation, the mailing of the films to the stations, and the correspondence with them concerning the program. Jane Truax, a fine writer and good friend, wrote the scripts built around each day's lesson from *Daily Word*. Rod Friend, director of the department, made sure everything moved the way it was supposed to move.

Whenever I see "the church lady" on *Saturday Night Live*, I wonder if Dana Carvey had seen "The *Daily Word*" on TV when he was a child. I hope not. It's not a pleasant thought to think one might have been the original "church lady"!

"The *Daily Word*" was in syndication until the mid-sixties. In the beginning we were doing it day-and-date, according to the plan advocated by Lowell Fillmore, so that each day's lesson matched the one in the viewer's *Daily Word* magazine. It was the ideal way, but it was also a very costly way since each film got only one use.

Viewers liked the program, and stations liked it so well they actually allowed us to make a once-a-week one-minute pitch for monetary support—unheard of on free programming. Viewers responded to the extent that we received $21,000 in offerings the last week of day-and-date programs. But this was only a drop in the bucket compared to the actual cost of the show, which included making and mailing eighty-seven tapes a day to the stations.

We then shot a year's worth of shows that mentioned only the day of the week, not the date, and concealed the cover of the magazine. These were sent out as reruns. The program continued in this way for several years but was not as popular as before. By this time too, television was becoming more sophisticated, and it became much more difficult to find a home for free five-minute segments in the world of one-minute and thirty-second spots. Finally, the program was discontinued.

It was because of "The *Daily Word*" program that I received the invitation to go on the trip I wrote about earlier. It also reached more people than I realized, because whenever I spoke at Unity centers around the country, people recognized me and asked about the program.

I truly enjoyed the years I filmed "The *Daily Word*." The people who were involved in making it possible became dear friends, and together we had lots of fun making it happen. But change is inevitable, and it became time to move on.

Top: Rosalind in the early '70s.
Middle: Rick Grace around 1970.
Bottom: Stanley Grace, Rick and
Rosalind's father, around 1950.

# 11. An Ending and a Beginning

During the year I spent working in television with "The *Daily Word*" program, my professional life was great, but my personal life was not so good. Finally, after seventeen years of marriage, my husband and I decided to divorce. No one in my family had ever even considered divorce and to actually get one was just not an option. But I suppose in every family there is one who does the unimaginable. In our family, I was always the one who stepped across the line, broke the mold, jumped in when it might have been more prudent to stand still.

Stanley was a good man, but together we were like apples and oranges trying to grow on the same tree. It just was not nurturing for either of us. His focus was on his business and real estate, and mine was on Unity. We both cared deeply about our children, and that is why we tried for seventeen years to make our marriage work. It finally got to the point where we realized that for all of us it would be better if we separated. It was one of the most difficult decisions I have ever made, but I know it was the right one. Divorce is never easy, even in the best of circumstances, and for children it is especially difficult, no matter what their ages.

I know this was a painful time for my children, and I shall forever be grateful to them for the loving, courageous support they gave to both their parents when they must have been greatly concerned about their own futures. My two children never cease to inspire me. They are now in their middle years, and both of them are wonderful, responsible, loving human beings, whose maturity has always exceeded that of their parents. Rick and Rosalind have been my life's greatest blessing, and I thank God every day that I have been allowed to share my journey with these two beautiful souls.

Our divorce was an amicable one, and Stanley and I remained friends. When you share children there is a bond that must be honored, and both of us realized that.

After the divorce, I felt the need to take some time away from my work at Unity School. My dear friend Sue Sikking invited me to be with her at Unity by the Sea in Santa Monica, California. I had gotten to know Sue when she came to speak and teach at Unity Village.

Sue Sikking was an amazing woman. She was the mother of five children. She was the author of many successful books, including *A Letter to Adam* and *God Always Says Yes*. She was the minister of a large congregation in Santa Monica, where she built a beautiful church.

Sue's husband Arthur, whom everyone called Pop, was also an ordained Unity minister, and three of their children—Robert, Tom, and Joy—became Unity ministers too. Their oldest son, Art Jr., is retired from a successful business career. Their youngest son, James, is a fine actor whose film and television credits are too numerous to mention except to note that one of his most memorable roles was on the television series *Hill Street Blues*.

The most remarkable thing about Sue was that with all the demands that were made upon her time and energy, her spirit never seemed to flag, nor did she ever fail to reach out to those who came to her for spiritual help. Of all the ministers I have ever known, Sue was the most like my grandfather. She and Pop lived in a beautiful home that overlooked Santa Monica Bay, and like Papa Charlie, they always had someone living with them who needed a place to stay. Their guests might stay for a day or a year, but Sue and Pop would give them material and spiritual support as long as they were there. And that is exactly what they did with me.

I stayed in their home only a short time before finding my own place, but for one whole year I worked with Sue and Joy at Unity by the Sea. I say I worked, but in truth I didn't really do very much. I sat at the receptionist desk, talked with people, answered the phone, and did some other odd jobs; but mostly I observed Sue and Joy and learned firsthand what a multifarious occupation the ministry is. Many people in the film industry attended Unity by the Sea. Sue's congregation was filled with interesting people: actors, screenwriters, singers, technical people, and executives.

All the Sikkings were vibrant, exciting people, and

they welcomed me into their family with such warmth and love that I will always remember it as a very special time. Joy became like a sister to me and is one of my dearest friends.

During my year in Santa Monica I got to know my mother's youngest sister, who lived there. I had met my Aunt Marie before, but since she lived in California, I had not spent much time with her. She was a beautiful woman, who shared with me her memories of my mother and their childhood together in Kansas. It was good to have her in my life. I felt that at last I had a connection to my mother's family and her life before she married my father. Aunt Marie lived in Santa Monica until her death, and we stayed in close communication.

After staying with Pop and Sue for a few weeks, I found, through an ad in the paper, a lovely cottage built on a cliff overlooking the Pacific Ocean in Malibu. I had always dreamed of living by the sea, and this place was an answer to prayer. It had been built for a film actress of the thirties, Mary Astor, as her beach house. It was just one large room plus a bedroom, but everywhere you looked you saw the sea. Either Mary Astor or some other owner had named it Stella Maris, "Star of the Sea."

My daughter and I spent a year in this cottage that looked to the sea. My son was in his first year of college but would come for holidays. It was a year of healing and reflection. Rosalind attended Santa Monica High School, and I worked a few hours a day, as I said, at Sue's church.

For my daughter and me, it was a very different experience. We both had spent our lives in the Midwest, about as far from an ocean as you can be. I loved that little home by the sea. It was wonderful to take long walks on the beach, to watch the changing tides, and to feel the comforting, healing rhythm of the waves as they moved across the shore.

But the year passed quickly, and it became time for me to return to Unity Village and begin again.

Top: Ralph Rhea, Mrs. Robert Wagner, Robert Wagner,
   and Rosemary.
Bottom: Rosemary, Ralph, and Shirley Jones.

# 12. Hollywood and "The Word"

Soon after I returned to Unity after my year in California, the director of the Radio Department, Dr. Carl Frangkiser, retired. Besides being an outstanding band conductor, he had also for many, many years been responsible for broadcasting Unity messages on radio.

While I had been on television with "The *Daily Word*," Unity's radio outreach was a program called "Unity Viewpoint." But just as it was becoming difficult to get five-minute segments on TV for religious programming, it was also becoming difficult to buy five-minute segments on radio in good time slots for religious programming. When I was invited to become director of both Radio and Television for Unity after Dr. Frangkiser's retirement, it was my job to come up with an idea for how we were to continue broadcasting Unity messages in a rapidly changing industry.

After giving it much thought and prayer, an idea came to me. If the stations didn't want religious programming, why not give them the same philosophy which had been expressed with so much appeal in "The *Daily Word*" on TV and by "Unity Viewpoint" on radio? Only this time put it in secular language and say it in sixty seconds, and then make the spots so attractive to the broadcasters that they couldn't resist playing them. How do you make them irresistible?—by having a celebrity be the spokesperson.

There are times in our lives when an idea comes to us that is so clear, so complete that we have no doubt that it's right. And this is how "The Word From Unity" came into my mind. I remember sitting in my office on the fourth floor of the Tower, pondering how we were going to get Unity's message on the airwaves, and it was as if someone started writing on a blackboard in my mind: "In the beginning was the Word" (Jn. 1:1). So why not call the spots "The Word From Unity" and then write scripts, find some celebrities, record them, and begin sending audition tapes to radio stations? It was all there in a flash. The map had been drawn; but scripts, celebrities, and stations were down the road a piece.

As I planned my new work, I discovered that Ralph Rhea had also returned to the Village to work in the Education Department as dean of Administration. Ralph's path and mine had not crossed since he had left the School a number of years before to become a minister of a church in Florida. I was surprised to learn that he, too, had recently been divorced and was beginning a new era of his life just as I was. I was sorry that his marriage, like mine, had not worked out. Ralph and I had always been good friends, and it was pleasing to know that he was back at Unity. After a while Ralph and I began going to movies and to dinner as friends do. After a year or so, we realized that not only had we become best friends, but we also cared very deeply for each other. On March 29, 1968, we were married, and the happiest period of my adult life began. Everything was right. I was married to a man I loved and respected, and I was involved in work I truly enjoyed.

Ralph's two children, Bonnie and Pete, were now grown up and married with families of their own. Pete Rhea is a Unity minister, like his father, and at the present time is serving at Unity Church of Bellingham in Washington. Pete and his beautiful wife Theresa are an integral part of my life, and I love them dearly, as I do Bonnie and her husband Jerry, who live in Canton, North Carolina. Ralph was extremely proud of his children, and rightly so; they are fine people who have blessed my life in so many ways. At the time Ralph and I married, my two children were in college. Ralph was a supportive, caring father and an outstanding grandfather. Because he had his own inner struggles, Ralph was an especially compassionate, insightful counselor.

Soon after our marriage, Ralph left the Education Department to join me in developing "The Word." The spots had already started on radio and were being well received by the stations. But if we were to expand into television, it was going to take a lot of creativity and ingenuity to figure out how we could film the stars in California and do the scripting, editing, and distribution at Unity Village, for we were operating within a very small budget. Plus—and this was a big plus—we had to find the stars. To find stars you have to go where they shine, and that of course was in Hollywood. Ralph at that time didn't like to fly and insisted that the only way he would go with me on my search for celebrities was if we drove. That was why we drove all the way from Missouri to California.

We arrived in Los Angeles late in the afternoon. We had no reservations, and we didn't have a clue as to where we were going to find celebrities to do spots for us—particularly since we were going to ask them to *donate* their time and talent. But somehow we both knew it was going to work out. As they say, "Fools rush in."

There we were, two tired travelers driving up Sunset Boulevard, when I saw a small sign that read "Bel-Air Hotel," with an arrow pointing down Stone Canyon Drive. I immediately got excited.

When my daughter and I lived in Malibu, we used to drive through Bel-Air to see the lovely homes. Frequently we would pass by the Bel-Air Hotel, an elegant hideaway for the rich and acclaimed, and I would fantasize about someday staying there. When I saw the sign, I said: "Ralph, slow down! There is a sign that says the Bel-Air Hotel is down the road on the left. I've always wanted to stay there. Let's see if they have a room for just one night."

He looked at me as if I had truly lost my mind. He then patiently began explaining, as though he were speaking to an unreasonable child, that it would be much too expensive, even if they would consider allowing a couple of frazzled people from Missouri without reservations to rent a room for just one night. I should just forget it— surely there was a Howard Johnson's around somewhere. But I persisted: "Let's just try. Maybe we could afford one night. It would be an adventure, and even if we don't get in, at least we would have seen what it looks like." I think just to get me off his back, Ralph finally relented. He turned the car around and followed Stone Canyon Drive to the lovely entrance of the Bel-Air Hotel.

The parking attendant was friendly. He didn't seem distressed by our dirty car or our rumpled appearance. Ralph, with great reluctance, went into the hotel to see about a room while I waited in the car. My bravado, you see, had faded when we actually got to the hotel. I persuaded Ralph he should go in by himself because he could handle rejection better than I could! By this time, I imagine, he was so tired of me and my nagging insistence on this crazy plan that he was glad to leave me in the car; that way he could quickly get in and out of the hotel, and we could get on with finding a suitable motel.

After he had been gone for what seemed a long time, he came out smiling from ear to ear. We not only had a room, but it was almost as if they had been expecting us. It seemed that practically everyone who worked at the hotel read the *Daily Word*. Mrs. Robert Wagner Sr., the mother of the well-known movie actor of that name, was a permanent resident of the hotel, and she gave all the employees gift subscriptions to the magazine. It was as though some good fairy had just handed us the magic key that opened doors in the enchanted kingdom of Hollywood!

The Bel-Air's manager introduced us to Mrs. Wagner. She was a lovely, gracious lady who looked amazingly like her handsome son. It was obvious that he had inherited his good looks from his mother. She told us that she had been a *Daily Word* reader for many years and always gave it as a gift to as many friends as possible.

Mrs. Wagner not only introduced us to her son Robert, who volunteered to do a television spot for us, but she continued to be very supportive of our project during the years we traveled to Los Angeles to film "The Word." Mrs. Wagner and I became good friends, and we kept in touch with each other until she made her transition some years later.

She was to the Bel-Air Hotel what Eloise was to the Plaza.[18] She was very discreet, but I'm pretty sure she knew everything that was happening at the hotel, and the employees loved her. The best table was always kept for her in the restaurant, and because we were her friends, we were given special consideration also.

One day she invited us to have lunch with her daughter-in-law, Natalie Wood. The famous actress was very beautiful and seemingly rather shy. On the other hand, she may have just been bored, although she was very gracious. I'll bet she was wondering why she had been invited to have lunch with people with whom she had so little in common.

Top: Barbara Feldon and Ralph.
Bottom: Ralph, Ralph Pabien, and Martin Landau.

Natalie's tragic death was a heartbreaking experience for Robert Wagner and his family. Why people have to experience such tragedy is inexplicable, but there must be reasons that only our soul knows and perhaps at some point in time we will understand why every experience is a necessary part of our journey.

Because of Mrs. Wagner's friendship, I'm sure, the Bel-Air Hotel was kind enough to allow us to do our filming on its grounds. The lovely Spanish architecture looked very much like some of the buildings at Unity Village, so when we edited the TV spots there was a harmonious flow between those filmed at the Bel-Air and those filmed at the Village.

It was an amazing time. After our initial journey to California, we returned to the Bel-Air twice a year for some ten years. On one trip, we would bring our soundman, Mark Weddle, to record radio spots; on the other trip, a small film crew from Kansas City would accompany us to do the filming for TV.

One door after another opened to us, and a remarkable number of well-known personalities helped us with our project. However, the two people who really got us started with the television spots were Jayne Meadows and Steve Allen. Jayne had been a longtime *Daily Word* reader, so she and Steve volunteered to do two spots for us more or less as a pilot so that the television stations and the people at Unity could see what they would be like. Unity School thought they were wonderful, and the stations we sent them to also responded with enthusiasm. We were on our way.

Jayne and Steve were also enormously helpful in getting many of their friends in the industry to film spots. In fact, I will never forget the lovely party they gave at their house for Ralph and me and a number of the celebrities that had filmed spots for "The Word."

My dinner partners that night were Dave Garroway on one side and Ernest Borgnine on the other, and I kept thinking, Is this really happening? Dave Garroway confided to me that when he was hosting *The Today Show* he had been very impressed by Anne Francis when he met her in New York, but their paths had not again crossed until this night. And he expressed to me how very pleased he was that she was at this party. Anne was a popular television actress in the sixties and seventies and had been kind enough to do a number of spots for "The Word." She was interested in Unity and had been a visitor at the Village. Anne was a very attractive woman, and I could understand Mr. Garroway's interest.

Another guest at the party was Ed Asner. I had always liked Mr. Asner. He played his role as Mary's boss on the *Mary Tyler Moore Show* with great wit and charm. I was delighted to discover that evening that he was also a native Kansas Citian.

Steve and Jayne introduced us to many wonderful people in the entertainment industry, and I shall always be grateful for all they did for us and for Unity. Steve Allen was a multitalented person—comedian, composer, musician, author, and producer. On television, he was a very funny, genial host; but in person, he was a quiet, reflective man who always carried with him a small cassette recorder so he could record any thought or idea that he wanted to remember. Steve also had great appreciation of talent, and many young comedians, musicians, and singers got their start on his *Tonight Show*.

Another memorable evening was a party my good friend Mala Powers had for some of the people who had done "The Word" spots plus some of her friends who lived in the neighborhood. One of them happened to be Jonathan Winters. The thing I remember best about that evening was Steve Allen quietly sitting at the piano, softly playing background music as the other guests visited with one another. And then every once in a while Jonathan Winters would take center stage and begin ad-libbing one of his many, many characters. Steve would stop playing and start laughing so hard that I thought he was going to fall off the piano bench. Jonathan Winters is one of the cleverest, funniest comedians alive, and Steve's great appreciation of his talent must have been very heart-warming to Mr. Winters.

Imagine a party where background music is played by Steve Allen and comic relief is supplied by Jonathan Winters—a combination any hostess would die for. Mala must have felt very good about her party; I know I did.

On one of our trips to Los Angeles, the Allens took

us out for dinner to a small, intimate restaurant in Beverly Hills. I don't remember its name, but I do remember its clientele. On the way to our table, Jayne and Steve were stopped by George Burns, who was seated nearby. As Steve and Mr. Burns chatted, I kept thinking that in the last movie I had seen George Burns had played God. In fact, I think he played God in three movies. He seemed to be a sweet, kind man and had a great sense of humor—all attributes one would hope God would have if He appeared in human form—so it is not surprising that some casting director must have leaped with joy when George Burns agreed to play a Hollywood screen writer's fanciful God. Everyone who saw the movie loved him. He was warm, human, funny—the kind of God we would all like to have as our best friend.

After dinner, as we were about to leave, Steve spotted Ethel Merman sitting across the room. She motioned for us to come over to her table and invited us to sit down for a moment. When Jayne and Steve explained that we were from Unity, her face lit up and she smiled that magnetic Merman smile and exclaimed: "I love Unity! I'm never without the *Daily Word.*" We started talking, and she asked if we had ever considered doing a television special, featuring entertainers who were interested in Unity. We replied that we hadn't thought of that, but it was a wonderful idea. Jayne and Steve agreed that Unity should consider doing a special since the three people sitting at that table would love to be part of such a project.

Think about it—Steve Allen, Jayne Meadows, and Ethel Merman volunteering their time and talents! It was an exciting prospect, but unfortunately, soon after that evening, we left the School and it never happened.

It was also the Allens who introduced us to Janet and Robert Lee, and they, too, were extremely helpful in contacting friends they knew who read the *Daily Word*. One was Harriet Nelson of *The Ozzie and Harriet Show*. My kids had grown up watching the Nelson family, and it was such a privilege to meet Harriet Nelson and to have her record "The Word" for Unity.

Another couple who were a tremendous help in getting well-known people for our spots were Bonita Granville Wrather and her husband Jack. Bonita had been a child actress appearing in many films, including *Hitler's Children*. Jack was a Texas oil baron turned Hollywood producer. Their best-known series was *Lassie*. Although Bonita was Catholic, she was an ardent *Daily Word* reader; she and Jack always started their day with it. Bonita and Jack became our good friends and visited us in Kansas City.

There were so many people in the industry who assisted us with "The Word." The list of celebrities that gave so generously of their talents is incredible: people like Wayne Rogers, of *M.A.S.H.* fame; Irene Dunn, a star of the thirties and forties; Susan Sullivan; Bernadette Peters; Johnny Mathis; Lou Rawls; Della Reese; Lloyd and Beau Bridges; Robert Stack; Diane Ladd; Nanette Fabray; Ida Lupino; Phyllis Diller; James Sikking; Ned Beatty;

Richard Bach, author of *Jonathan Livingston Seagull*; Bob Barker; Joe Campanello; Robert Wagner; Vera Miles; Shirley Jones; Audrey Meadows; Pearl Bailey; Eddie Albert; Rosalind Russell—and these are just a few!

I do want to tell you a story about Rosalind Russell. Ms. Russell had invited us to her home to record a radio spot. As a kid, I had always been a big fan of hers, and I was in awe that I was going to actually meet her. When we arrived, she was very charming and very much as she was in her films. While we were setting up the equipment, the telephone rang; when she answered, it was impossible not to hear her side of the conversation. It was Frank Sinatra calling. It seemed that he was a very good friend of Rosalind and her husband, and the previous night he had serenaded them under their window at 2 a.m. Now he was calling to apologize for waking them up. Wow, I thought, Imagine having Frank Sinatra singing under your window and then calling to apologize! I had a girl friend when I was in high school who stood in line in freezing rain for hours upon hours just to catch a glimpse of him when he came to Kansas City. He was the teenage idol of my generation. And now, years later, I was sitting in Rosalind Russell's living room listening as she scolded Frank Sinatra for disturbing her sleep! I wonder if she had any idea how many millions of women in America would have thought they were in heaven if they were awakened by his singing beneath their window—no matter what the hour.

Publicists for the stars were also especially helpful to

us in our pursuit of well-known people. We discovered that Hollywood is actually a rather small community, and word travels fast as to who is doing what. So when it became known that several celebrities were participating in our project, publicists began calling us to suggest that some of their clients would be interested in filming "The Word."

One of the publicists was particularly helpful in the beginning. Judy was a very attractive woman, and the one and only time I have ever fixed up anyone with a blind date was with Judy and Terry Paulson. You will recall Terry was the son of my very dear friends Jane and Sig Paulson, and when we were at the Village, Terry came by our home one night to tell us that he was being transferred to Los Angeles. Did we know anyone there he might enjoy meeting? I immediately thought of Judy and gave him her telephone number. When Terry got to Los Angeles he called her, and the next time I heard from Terry and Judy they were planning their marriage! You never know what role you may play in someone else's life journey. Just because I handed Terry a phone number, two lives were completely changed. Our lives are full of such tiny acts that are like pebbles cast into a pool, making ripples that spread to alter life's patterns in innumerable ways—many of which we will never know. After their marriage, they moved to Seattle, Washington, and Judy never returned to her work as a film publicist.

Our Hollywood years were extraordinary. The entertainment industry is extremely generous in supporting projects that they deem worthy. It was amazing to know that *Daily Word* magazine reached into so many Hollywood homes and that its daily messages were read by all those gifted, creative people. It truly was the magic key that made "The Word From Unity" a reality.

At the same time we were doing "The Word," our department also produced two films: *Charles Fillmore: American Mystic* and *Unity, a School of Christianity*. These films were written, directed, and edited by Rick Grace, my son, who joined the department after graduating from the University of Missouri. After Ralph and I left Unity School, Rick continued working in the Radio and Television Department until he left to become director of the Cassettes Department. Eventually, however, Rick left Unity School to establish his own audiovisual company.

My years spent working in radio and television were the greatest; but as I have said, "for everything there is a season, and a time for every purpose," and my media season seemed to have fulfilled its purpose.

# 13. The Ministry

One occupation that was not on my list of possible career options was the ministry. The ministry, in my mind, was a calling rather than something you chose as a profession. I had never been called into the ministry, nor did I have any desire to be called.

All my life I had been surrounded by ministers. Most of my friends were ministers, and I was married to a minister; so I fully realized what a demanding occupation the ministry is. I don't think the average person realizes how many roles good ministers are called upon to play. To name just a few: they must be good public speakers, teachers, counselors, administrators, fundraisers, arbitrators. They are required to perform weddings, funerals, christenings, spiritual communion, hospital and bereavement calls, and in small churches they sweep the floor and take out the trash—and that's just a short list of the jobs ministers must do!

One time a minister friend told me that at a church board meeting where the possibility of increasing the minister's salary was being discussed, one member remarked, "Well, I don't see why you should receive more money; you only work on Sunday mornings!"

I keep an office at Unity in the Education Department, and when I see the ministerial students happily going to their classes I wonder if they have any conception of what an exacting profession they have chosen. I think few do, for the attrition rate in the first few years of actual ministry is great.

When Ralph and I decided to accept Mary Kupferle's invitation to come to Unity of Delray Beach in 1980, Ralph thought it would be good if I would become an ordained minister since we both were going to be working in a church together. I had taken courses in the ministerial school, not to become a minister, but because I wanted to explore the Unity teachings more deeply. Because of my years of work in Unity and because I had taken so many Unity classes, the Association of Unity Churches allowed me to be ordained through their Special Ordination Program. But it was still not in my mind that I would ever be a "pulpit" minister. I would simply assist Ralph and Mary in doing whatever was needed at the church. I particularly enjoyed leading prayer groups and meditations. Ralph was the one who was real help to Mary. I was sort of along for the ride.

As it happened, we were in Delray Beach for only six months when we were called and asked to be the ministers at the Unity Church of Port Richey in Florida. We were not happy about leaving Delray Beach, but Ralph felt that we should accept the invitation since Mary really didn't need us and Port Richey was without a minister. So we moved to Florida's west coast.

Soon after our arrival in Port Richey, Ralph experienced a mild stroke, and it was necessary for him to take time for rest and recuperation. It seemed to me that the best thing we could do was to return to Kansas City since I had no experience in running a church, but the church board insisted that we stay. They said they would help me run the church until Ralph could return to work. They were so insistent and so encouraging we couldn't say no. Suddenly I became the minister of a church with a congregation of approximately 500 people without a clue of how I was going to manage it. I had never done a wedding or a funeral, and the thought of getting up every Sunday and giving a sermon was beyond my imagination even though I had been a visiting speaker many times.

Somehow I muddled through. However, it was possible only because I was blessed by a wonderful caring board, whose president, Lois Newbrand, was helpful in every way, as were all the board members. My sweet, beautiful administrative assistant, Lynn, kept the office running smoothly, and the congregation was so tolerant and supportive that it would have been difficult to fail. I shall forever be grateful to the previous minister, Philip Smeadstead, who had been the minister when this beautiful church was being built and had left it in perfect order. With the help of all the wonderful people in Unity Church of Port Richey what could have been a miserable time turned into one of the most uplifting and important experiences of my adult life. I will forever be grateful to each person there who put up with my inexperience as I learned how to be a minister.

I shall never forget the first wedding at which I officiated, and I'm sure the same is true of the bride and groom. Fortunately, it was a very small wedding, just the bride and groom and two witnesses. Frightened that I would make a mistake, I was shaking so much I could barely hold the prayer manual. Finally I had to stop in the middle of the ceremony and ask the bride and groom if they would mind if I sat down! I was thinking that if I didn't sit down I might fall down. They looked at each other in amazement and nodded their consent, and I finished the wedding ceremony sitting in a chair. It was one of the most embarrassing experiences of my life. I never saw the poor bride and groom again. I pray that their marriage was more successful than their wedding!

My first funeral was almost as bad. When I got to the funeral home, the director found it hard to believe I was the officiating minister and kept trying to seat me in the pew reserved for the family. This didn't help my confidence any, and it certainly needed help. I remember looking down at the casket and thinking, At least you don't have to get up in front of a group of strangers and preach a eulogy when you're scared half out of your wits; you must be in a better place!

Weddings and funerals never became easy for me. I always felt somewhat like an impostor posing as a minister and that the bride and groom or the bereaved deserved someone with better spiritual credentials to officiate on such important occasions.

We had hoped Ralph's health would improve, but this did not happen. Finally, after a couple of years had passed, we decided it was best that we move back to the Kansas City area to be near our family.

After returning home, we opened a small church which we named the Unity—Myrtle Fillmore Center. This little church eventually merged with Unity Temple on the Plaza, and Duke Tufty, who was minister of the Myrtle Fillmore Center after I returned to Unity School, then became minister of Unity Temple on the Plaza. With Duke as its spiritual leader, along with Karyn Bradley, Unity on the Plaza is now one of the largest, most vibrant churches in the Unity movement.

For me, church ministry, although challenging, was also extremely rewarding. I was pushed to do things I had never dreamed of doing, and I discovered that we are all much more capable than we think we are.

The best part of ministry for me, and what I miss most, was connecting with people. It has been said that we are all heroes in search of a role, and during my years in the ministry, I met many heroes—men and women who quietly went about their lives as they moved courageously through adversities that would test the bravest of us. There are so many good people in our world that it is hard to understand why we humans have such difficulty living in peace with one another.

Ralph and I experienced the same wonderful support when we began our little church in Kansas City as we did in Florida. My dear friends Frank and Martha Giudici were the ministers at the Unity Village Chapel at that time, and they did everything they could to help our ministry. They both taught classes for us, as did two other fine Unity ministers, Sallye Taylor and Hypatia Hasbrouck. Sallye Taylor introduced us to Geneva Price, a lovely Kansas City vocalist who eventually became our soloist, and to Mildred Johnson, a beautiful, faith-filled lady who became the leader of our prayer ministry. Hypatia brought us Michael Davenport, a talented writer and radio producer, who was also a good musician. Michael not only played the piano for us, he also wrote and produced for the Myrtle Fillmore Center a series of award-winning public service spots called "Dare."

It was many talented people coming together to form a spiritual community that made the Myrtle Fillmore Center a viable, active ministry. People like Pam Yearsley, who was at that time editor of *Unity Magazine*; Al Tilton, TWA pilot and a great piano player; and my good, good friends Merle and Bill Moores, who gave me the courage to pioneer a church. There are so many individuals who were vitally important in creating this ministry that it would be impossible to name them all. Good friends came from around the country to bless our church. Wally Amos, Dr. Jerry Jampolsky, Walter Starcke, and Jack Boland lectured at the Myrtle Fillmore Center without compensation because they wanted to help.

It was a community effort, and we became a close spiritual family. I believe all of those who worked together to build the center understood how much they contributed to its success. I hope they know, because it was their energy and their love that created that little spiritual haven called the Unity—Myrtle Fillmore Center. It was a special place and our time together for me was a very special time. I hope it was the same for all of those who made it happen.

One thing became very clear to me during my years in the ministry: many of us are stuck in a groove, and like a broken record, we keep repeating the same problems over and over, year in and year out, until we finally awaken to what life is trying to teach us. We are like the man in the movie *Groundhog Day*. We keep repeating the same behavioral pattern, expecting different results and are dismayed when, instead, we find ourselves experiencing the same challenges today that we were experiencing yesterday. This is not only true of individuals but also of nations and even civilizations. History proves that if we refuse to learn from past misconceptions we are doomed to repeat them.

Isn't it time that we stop repeating our painful past and, instead, choose at last to follow the path so clearly marked for us by the most enlightened revolutionary in the history of our world? Isn't it time we choose love?

"This is my commandment, that you love one another as I have loved you" (Jn. 15:12).

Around the world in 1962 with Rosemary Grace. "This I know with all my heart and soul," she said. "That this world needs Unity more than it needs anything else. It needs our prayers and it needs our ideas."

# 14. Unity in the Twenty-First Century

M ost would agree that we are living in extraordinary times. September 11, 2001, was a pivotal moment in history—not only the history of America or the world but of civilization as a whole. However, even before September 11, I believe thinking people realized that the rapid advances being made by science and technology were leading humanity to a place where our collective spiritual and moral choices would greatly influence the future of our planet. September 11 was a tragic wake-up call, and we were left with the perplexing question of how we are going to answer it, individually and collectively.

The first Sunday after that unbelievable September day, people crowded into churches seeking solace and reassurance. It was like Christmas and Easter combined; there were no empty pews. The Christian world came together in prayer. As they used to say during World War II: "There are no atheists in foxholes." We turn to religion when we are feeling threatened and anxious; and heretofore, the world's religions have provided the spiritual answers we seek when things happen that are beyond our human understanding.

Religion has provided the inspiration that has awakened humankind to the spiritual dimension of life. But religion has also been extremely divisive. As we view our world's history, we find that religion has been the root cause of many of the conflicts that have plagued our civilization. And now in the twenty-first century, it is religious extremists who are committing acts of violence in the name of God. In this century, some of the most established religions are being shaken to their foundations by inner conflict.

If we are to bring forth the millennium as described in Revelation, we must begin expressing a transcendent spirituality that supercedes the extreme biases of religiosity. This is not to say that we should all have the same belief system; to the contrary, it is the diversity of our search that makes our journey joyously and mysteriously adventurous. However, we are living in a time of revolution. Science and technology are leading us into incredible dimensions of new possibilities. Reality is rapidly outstripping science fiction and fantasy. The communications revolution, combined with the globalization of commerce and the speed of travel, has made us a global community whether we like it or not. What happens anywhere happens to us. And if we think we can put the genie back in the bottle, we had better think again: we *are* one world right now.

The old paradigms will not work in a changing universe. The challenges facing our world today cannot be solved in the same consciousness in which they have been created. Life is demanding that we think in higher categories. To survive as a human species, we must learn finally and forevermore that violence begets violence, and the eye-for-an-eye morality, as Gandhi so aptly said, ends in a world of darkness. The urgency of this time calls for a revolution of consciousness. Revolutionary times demand revolutionary thinking.

Charles Fillmore was a revolutionary thinker. We forget that sometimes because so many of the things he taught—like the role the mind plays in causing illness and the power of positive thinking, to mention two—are now widely accepted. But in the beginning, he was considered shocking and was often condemned by established religions.

He wrote: "All reforms must begin with their cause. Their cause is mind, and mind does all its work in the realm of silence, which, in reality, is the only realm where sound and power go hand in hand.... All philosophers and sages have recognized this silent cause, this perpetual outflow from center to circumference."[19]

The basic Truth that Unity propounds is that we have a world inside of us that is governed by principles, just as science is governed by principles; and if we become aware of these principles and apply them, we can change our lives. If we want to heal our outer world, we must first heal our inner nature.

When Charles Fillmore was meditating, the name

*Unity* was revealed to him by what he felt was divine guidance; surely he was right, because no name could be more appropriate for the central thrust of the movement or for the need of this particular time. Webster's *New World Dictionary* defines "unity" as "being united, oneness ... a complex that is a union of separate parts." This is the particular strength of Unity, that it seeks only inclusion, never the marking out of a territory. You do not have to give up any of your ideas to be a Unity student; Unity is a big umbrella. When I read mail at headquarters, I saw letters from nuns, ministers of other faiths, people from non-Christian countries—all practicing Unity beliefs. Certainly religion in the twenty-first century must honor its diverse expression while working together for the good of all people; this is Unity.

Because Unity began as a healing ministry and its main emphasis for over a hundred years has been on healing, it can play an important role in the great drama that is unfolding around us. For most of the last century, Unity had been on the cutting edge of "the consciousness movement." Today organized religion and science are in many instances at odds with each other; recent scientific discoveries seem to refute some of religion's fundamental teachings.

James Dillet Freeman writes of Unity's place in this conflict in his magazine column "Life Is a Wonder":

Religion, to meet the needs of a scientific

age or any age, has to have three elements:
(1) it has to be rationally acceptable, (2) it has
to be emotionally moving, and (3) it has to be
aesthetically satisfying....

The motivation of ... Charles and Myrtle
Fillmore ... was to find religious doctrines they
could accept in light of the new scientific
knowledge. They did not want to live without
religion.

But they ... also ... did not want to abandon their intelligence."[20]

It was their purpose to create a spiritual teaching
that was compatible with science.

In fact, Charles Fillmore prophesied that Unity
would become a connecting link between science and
religion, and his prophecy is beginning to take form. Sir
John Templeton, who, like Charles Fillmore, is seeking
ways to bring science and religion together, brought to
Unity Village some time ago a group of prominent theologians and scientists to discuss how science and religion can come together to improve our world. Hopefully,
this was just the first of many future meetings where creative minds join in unity to seek new ways to move our
planet forward.

Charles Fillmore was also one of the first religious
leaders to use the airwaves to communicate his message.
Today, with the advent of the information highway, the

possibilities of sending Unity's message of the healing power of love and forgiveness around our world are mind-boggling.

If the communication industry began using its amazing potential in positive ways, it could help impressionable young minds to understand the futility of violence instead of perpetuating it through the glorification of brutality and destructive behavior, which is such an integral part of most of the films, television programs, and computer and video games that America not only watches but exports to countries around the globe. It is time the multimedia conglomerates begin to act responsibly and use their great power to enhance the human experience rather than diminish it.

Writers, producers, artists, and programmers should be encouraged to use their creativity to find ways to make peace as exciting as war—conflict resolution more interesting than brute force. Why can't there be computer and video games where if you kill, you lose?

I visualize Unity Village establishing a spiritual "think-tank" where the brightest, most creative minds meet to explore how we can best inspire human beings to bring forth their infinite potential.

If you walk into any bookstore, you will find many books written by the so-called New Age writers, and many of their books have been on the best-seller lists. These New Age gurus have found some of their most receptive audiences in Unity churches. And if the best-seller list and the prices people pay to attend lectures and seminars featuring these transformation writers and lecturers are a gauge of what people are seeking, it would seem to reflect a great longing in the soul of America for a new religion, a new spirituality, because the old ways are not working in our conflicted, fragmented society.

Unity has played, and is playing, a very important role in consciousness change. At the present time new people are assuming leadership positions in Unity, and it is my prayer that they will realize the importance of following the path that Myrtle and Charles marked out for us as spiritual pioneers always on the frontier of faith. Unity must continue to explore new dimensions, examine new paradigms, and invite the most illumined, the most inspired, to share their insights. Otherwise, it will eventually dissolve into history as just another theological experiment that became irrelevant in a changing universe. Without vision—a nation, a people, or a spiritual movement perishes.

It is my belief that Unity will fulfill its destiny. I believe the same Spirit that inspired the Fillmores and those who followed them is guiding Unity today. We have the most needed message in our world. Unity's message is one of healing, of transcendence, of coming together. It is a message of empowerment, a message of infinite possibilities.

All around our globe people are yearning to feel God's love, to experience God's peace. Unity's primary purpose is to awaken people to the love that is in the

Truth of their being and to help them discover and use the power within them.

Over one million people each day are reading *Daily Word*. It is printed in seven languages and constitutes a magnificent prayer network that reaches around the globe. If that prayer network is increased each year by one or two million, think what a powerful impact it will have on world consciousness.

Students from distant lands are now in the Ministerial Education Program at Unity School. And I have a dream that we will soon have an international Unity corps, where teaching teams will go to Unity churches and study groups in other countries to give support to ministries that are just beginning. I also dream that we will have sister churches—as there are sister cities—to develop exchange programs which will provide opportunities for us to learn from one another.

One hundred years ago Myrtle Fillmore asked, "Who will take care of the children?" I wonder what she would think today when the great American tragedy has been kids killing kids, and now it is being seen in other countries as well. Unity's ministry to our young people is vitally important. We must translate our message into a language that reaches young people who are feeling lost and hopeless. We must help them understand and believe that their lives do have meaning and purpose.

One of the most exciting projects happening today in Unity was conceived by two inspired Texas gentlemen,

Frank Abraham and Neal Carson. It is called the Peace by Piece Program. Through this program, young people from around the world come to Unity Village to attend the Youth of Unity Conference each year. For two weeks these teenagers join with their American counterparts in sharing experiences, having fun, attending spiritual workshops, and most important establishing friendships that will remain long after they return to their respective countries. It is a life-changing experience for all who participate in this inspiring project.

In 1998 the International Youth of Unity officers represented the youth of the world at the United Nations, when The Global New Thought Alliance joined with the Martin Luther King Foundation and The Gandhi Foundation to launch "A Season for Nonviolence" to be held each year in the 64 days between Gandhi's assassination on January 30 and Martin Luther King's assassination on April 4. The Youth of Unity officers received a standing ovation after their presentation to the United Nations gathering. It was a moment I'm sure they will never forget, nor will those of us who were fortunate enough to be present.

I took my grandson Jacob with me on the trip to the United Nations, and he got to meet Gandhi's grandson, Arun Gandhi, as well as two of his great-great-grandsons, who were approximately Jacob's age. This was an exciting event for me. I remembered standing at Gandhi's tomb and seeing how people had used flowers to outline the letters of his name. I remembered, too, that Mahatma

Gandhi was a contemporary of Charles Fillmore. At the same time the Fillmores were creating their spiritual community in America, Gandhi was doing the same thing in South Africa, later moving his work to India.

Gandhi had been influenced by Leo Tolstoy, who also had a dream of making his farm a spiritual community. Gandhi had become aware of Tolstoy when he was attending school in England, where friends invited him to a meeting of Tolstoy's followers. Three inspired men in such divergent places as the American Midwest, Russia, and South Africa began creating communities with a similar spiritual purpose. And now decades later there is Unity Village in the United States, Unity Tolstoy Center in Russia, and Gandhi's commune in India. Arun Gandhi and I shared the platform at the 1999 Youth of Unity Conference at Unity Village.

I'm convinced that there is a circle of spiritual energy in our universe that is penetrated by inspired minds, and similar ideas are revealed to them, even though they have no knowledge of one another.

Each year the young people who have traveled to the conference as a part of the Peace by Piece Program present a program for the conference body. Approximately thirty countries are represented. At the 2001 summer conference, a young man from the South American country of Colombia told as his part of the program of the difficulty of maintaining a normal life in a country that is being ravaged by guerilla warfare and drug trafficking. He spoke of a friend who recently committed suicide because he could no longer handle his feelings of despair and hopelessness. When Jose was speaking about his friend, his voice filled with emotion and it was difficult for him to continue; but he did, and he closed his talk by beseeching his audience to please be kind to one another, for you never know just how much pain a friend may be experiencing. Six hundred teenagers were so still as Jose spoke that you literally could have heard a pin drop. He followed his talk with one of the most effective peace meditations I have ever been privileged to hear—and believe me, when I tell you I have heard a *lot* of meditations!

After the meditation, the Peace by Piece Program closed with a sweet Jamaican boy singing Bob Marley's "One Love." As he began to sing, every young person in the activity center spontaneously rose in unison, reached for their neighbors' hands, and began singing with him. It was an unforgettable moment, and for me it exemplified what Unity is all about.

In that moment I saw the future, and it was very good.

# Jamaica—April 2002

Soon I will be leaving Jamaica. I have been summoned home like an errant child who failed to come in from recess. And it is true: the child in me is reluctant to leave Jamaica. The simplicity of living here makes the thought of dress codes, schedules, strategic planning meetings, crowded freeways, and long lines at airports something not to look forward to.

The dress code here requires only shorts and T-shirts, bare feet or sandals. The strategic planning only concerns deciding if there will be fish or chicken for dinner, and that decision is actually determined by the sea. If the sea is calm, the fishermen are able to go to sea and check their nets; if the sea is rough, it's chicken for dinner. "No problem, mon."

Schedules are based on time, and I soon learned after my arrival here that there is American time and Jamaican time. Jamaican time is a creative individualistic expression. "Soon come back," a common parting phrase here, could mean, I will return in a few minutes, hours, days, or years. When a person leaves you with "Soon

215

come back," you can only wonder when you will see him or her again. After you overcome your initial frustration, you learn to live on Jamaican time, which is explained by another colloquialism: "Nothing happens before its time." And so Jamaicans come and go as their spirit moves them, and they believe you must honor your spirit. Somehow I don't think corporate America would empathize with this philosophy! It took me a while to adapt to Jamaican time, but now that I have, I find it a very relaxing, refreshing way of life. People here never seem perturbed if you are late or even if you fail to arrive at all! I know when I am home I will have to return to American time, for I doubt that my associates there would be quite so tolerant. Punctuality is a fundamental principle that must be honored if you are to be a part of the American way of life, but Jamaica is different.

On the positive side, I am looking forward to being once again with my family and friends. Although my family and many of my Unity friends have visited me in Jamaica, I have missed living close to those I love.

I know that I will return to Jamaica, not only because of my deep affinity for this beautiful island but also because my work here is not finished. The Unity Kindergarten and Preparatory School is filled to overflowing, and children are being turned away because there is no way to expand their present facility to bring more children into the school. The classrooms are filled to capacity. The children need more space between desks, and a cooler, more comfortable learning environment. They also need a playground for their recreational activities. At the present time their recess play must be done within the confines of a very small paved asphalt courtyard that has only a gate to separate it from a busy street. These beautiful Jamaican children deserve better facilities, and so do Pearl Davis and her wonderful staff of teachers. I know that I must return to Jamaica to help the Unity Faith Center in Montego Bay find the land and the means to build a school that would better exemplify the Unity principles these children are being taught. No child should have to be turned away from school because there is no room in the inn.

In my mind's eye, I see a lovely, simple building whose classrooms open to the out-of-doors so that the soft sea breezes can blow gently through the rooms to cool and soothe the children as they study. The school I visualize sits on an expanse of green grass, where children can run and play with no fear of skinned knees or congested traffic. In the distance is the sea, always the sea, a reminder of the ever-moving, ever-changing energy of life, but forever the sea.

I know that Unity Faith School is going to be built; I just don't know when or how. I just know that it is, and I ask you, dear reader, to know this with me. When it is built, other such schools around the globe will follow, so more and more children can become aware of the life-changing power within them even as they are educated in the more mundane subjects. Education is of primary importance if we are to bring forth a revolution of consciousness.

I have written this book for my two grandsons, Jacob and Adam Tanner. I want them to know about the people who created this spiritual movement we call Unity. I see in Jacob and Adam many of the qualities that were in their great-grandparents. Just as my dad and my Uncle Lowell were different from each other, so are brothers Jacob and Adam.

Jacob is a music major in his senior year of college. He was born with an adventurous spirit and began traveling the world at only eight years old, when he went with me to Russia. This was just the first of many, many trips we took together throughout his childhood. He has visited me here in Jamaica many times, just as Adam has. Jacob, however, resonates with Jamaica in the same way I do, while Adam prefers the mountains and a cooler climate.

Adam is truly a child of the twenty-first century. His computer is his lifeline to the world, and he is not content if he strays too far from it. Jacob perhaps would have been more comfortable being a part of the sixties generation. His favorite book is *Zen and the Art of Motorcycle Maintenance*. He is happy when he is here in Jamaica just playing his guitar or going to the fishing village with Devon to sit by the sea and visit with the Rasta fishermen. He shuns materialism and has become mostly a vegetarian. Besides his passion for music, he has taken an inordinate number of philosophy courses in college and is very interested in environmental issues. Jacob is a

Rosalind's family: son Adam, husband Eric, Rosalind, son Jacob.

resourceful, creative person who insists on following his "bliss," and isn't this the most important thing anyone can do? As Jamaicans say, "We must honor our spirit." If we don't, we may become outwardly successful but we miss the joy of the dance.

Adam is in his last year of high school. He is a handsome, intelligent young man who has a purity of spirit that is reminiscent of my Uncle Lowell's. His passion, as I said, is his computer while Jacob's is his music. Both have an equally important mission in our twenty-first-century world. Scientific projections for the future tell us that in fifteen to twenty years it will perhaps be possible to have dominion over the natural world—both inanimate and biological. And it is going to be people like Adam who are involved in computer science that will be a part of this amazing technological revolution. Charles Fillmore never feared science would destroy religion; he welcomed advances in science as part of the same overarching unity. We need this kind of thinking.

But Jacob's mission is equally important, for science must be balanced with our soul's need for transcendent experiences which come to us through music, art, religion, and nature. It is the artist's ability to find beauty and meaning in the ordinary and skillfully translate it into the extraordinary that illumines the human experience. Without art and artists, our world would be a stark and dreary place.

My grandsons illumine my world. They are two of the best things that have ever happened to me. I love my time with them. They are intelligent, fun, and tolerant of their grandmother's idiosyncrasies. The great thing about grandparenting is that you have all the joy without the responsibility that comes with parenthood. It's strange, but the older I get the younger and freer I feel inside. Perhaps that's why people talk about "second childhood," and perhaps that's also why grandparents relate so well with their grandkids. As you get older your priorities change. You find that things which seemed so important in one season of life are not that important in the next.

The principal thing that has made my stay in Jamaica such a beautiful time has been the people who have come to bless my life: Lorna, Linda, Mark, and Devon—my Jamaican family.

Since I first met Devon five years ago, he has

watched over me like an overly protective mother. People here call him my bodyguard (like I need a bodyguard?), but in truth, he is my guardian angel. He is a great cook and a good driver, and if you have ever driven in Jamaica, you know that good driving is not what Jamaicans are famous for. Every member of my family loves and appreciates Devon just as I do. Jacob calls him his other brother, and they have enjoyed many happy times together. Devon has been my Jamaican teacher. I'm sure that would surprise him, but I have learned so much about the Jamaican philosophy of life simply by observing and listening to Devon as he goes about his daily tasks.

Lorna Cheong is my beautiful friend. I tell her she is a walking United Nations. Her mother is Jamaican, her father was East Indian, and she was at one time married to a Chinese gentleman, hence the name Cheong. Lorna, like Devon, helps me in so many ways it would be impossible to list them all. I couldn't have remained in Jamaica without her loving assistance. Mark is her brother, and Linda is his partner. These three people have adopted me into their family. We celebrate birthdays, holidays, and Jamaican festivals together. I will miss these dear, dear friends when I return home, but I know: "Soon come back."

There is a place just outside of Montego Bay where I love to go. It is a beautiful spot on a hill that looks to the sea. Someone has placed a bench by the road so that passers-by may sit for a while as they stop to enjoy the view.

When I return to the Midwest and things get very

busy, I will go to that lovely spot in my mind. And I will remember the words of my young Jamaican teacher, Devon, who told me that when he is feeling confused about something he just sits down beneath a tree, closes his eyes, and lets the breeze blow through his mind.

So when I am home and the world is too much with me, I will close my eyes and let my spirit travel to that bench which looks to the sea, and I will feel the breeze gently blowing through my mind.

# Stella Maris
## "Star of the Sea" (1979)

Once when life was difficult, I began searching for a place to retreat. I was born and lived most of my life in the Midwest—far, far from the ocean—but deep within me I had always longed to live by the sea. Perhaps there is some past life that beckons me back. For whatever reason, my inner urging led me to the ocean, and I found Stella Maris—my home, my retreat, my haven by the sea. Stella Maris sits high on a bluff and looks to the sea. Whoever built this house, so aptly named it. Stella Maris means star of the sea, and at night the sea and the stars do meet here and rejoice with one another until the dawn.

The reflecting, the meditating, that I did the year I lived by the sea changed my life and, hopefully, as you read you will let go and give yourself to the sea as I did and it will do the same for you.

When I awoke this morning, Stella Maris was engulfed by fog. Every room has windows to the floor; so, wherever you look you see the sea except on days such as today when it is wrapped in misty clouds which are so dense that you see nothing beyond them. Listen: it is the sound of a foghorn of a passing ship. It seems to be crying: "Come with me. I will take you to new and exciting experiences, but you must hurry, because I can't wait long for you." I will not answer the call. I know now that wherever I go I take myself with me, and before I go again, I must find out who I am.

Why is self-reflection so difficult? Are we so afraid that what we might see would be so painful a picture of us that we could not bear to look at ourselves without the retouching and smooth finish we show the world? Or are we even more fearful that we would look within and find nothing there at all, that we are a mirage which disappears into the air as we step forward to explore ourselves. Whatever our fear may be, whatever drives us and keeps us running, this is the mirage and not ourselves. The mirage is fear.

The fears and anxieties that agonize us and rob us of our peace and happiness are usually intangible when we start to examine them. We fear failure; we fear loss that someone or something is going to steal from us that which is ours—whether it be love, money, or self-esteem. We fear illness and, most of all perhaps, we fear death. Fear is the devil. He has many synonyms, yet each of us hide and protect him with a strong cloth of our own imagination. Oh yes, we give him respectable names. We call him security, wisdom, safety, but by whatever name we call him, until we face him openly and honestly and realize that he has only the power we let him have, he will continue to steal from us our greatest treasure—the joy of living.

Life is an adventure and should be lived with a feeling of happy expectation instead of impending disaster. When I think about the people I know, even as I walk down the street and look into the face of strangers, I want to shout to them: "This is your life! Let go, relax, enjoy; there is nothing to be afraid of." Then fear turns his face to me as I catch a glimpse of my own image in a passing window, and I don't speak. We are such fools. We have been given the gift of life and instead of rejoicing, we let our fears and anxieties kill and destroy it for us. It is humanity's madness, inspired by the devil—fear.

The sea is high today. The waves shine, glisten, roar as they throw themselves against the rocks. It is as if they are shouting: "Look at us. We are strong, we are free, we are alive, we move with our moods, and today we feel beautiful and happy. Tomorrow we may be different, but we are the sea and you must accept us as we are. Why can't I be like that? If once and for all I could let go of my self-imposed limitations and let my real spirit express itself then I could be free like the waves of the sea. If I could cast aside the roles I play and accept myself as I am and others as they are, how wonderful it would be.

We spend so much of our lives building defenses. We think if people actually know us, they won't like or accept us. If we expose our weaknesses and our love, we feel vulnerable and open to too many possible hurts. The world has taught us this. No one likes to be hurt, but feeling pain is better than feeling nothing at all. Loving and losing are better than not loving at all. Trying and failing are better than standing still.

And what of others? If someone disappoints me or turns away, instead of crying or striking back, why can't I accept them as I do the sea? Okay, friend, you are rough and unapproachable now, and I will let you be. Perhaps another day, some other time we will meet again and our way will be smooth and clear.

One of the nicest parts of living by the sea is to watch the seagulls as they soar and swerve with the grace and freedom no human being possesses. They seem so free. *Free!* I have always thought this word to be one of the most beautiful in our language. The very sound of it draws to mind marvelous images. A bird flying gracefully against the tapestry of a blue, boundless sky, dipping and circling, waving as it flies on north or south as it chooses. The word *free* draws forth all kinds of glorious daydreams. It implies to be set loose from restraint or constraint—a permanent removal from whatever binds, confines, entangles, or oppresses. To be free from whatever binds, confines, entangles, or oppresses—ah, this is devoutly to be wished but rarely ever achieved.

In our complex world filled with people, technology, and problems, where would I begin to look for freedom? Must I travel to India and climb the Himalayas? Perhaps I'll find it on the psychiatrist's couch? But wherever I go, guru or psychiatrist, Shangri-La or the quiet of the analyst's office, the way is expensive and often remote. Is liberation then the ultimate luxury only for the very rich? No, now I remember "it is easier for a camel to go through the eye of a needle than for someone who is rich to enter the kingdom of God," and the wealthy can be as tied to their possessions, status, and power as the poor to their poverty. The kingdom of heaven is within you. Look into yourself.

So, where did my search for freedom lead me? In the beginning and in the end to myself.

The sea is angry today, the waves pound and pound against the shore as if they want to destroy the rocks and sand that only yesterday they were so gently caressing. Somewhere there was a bad storm, and the dark crashing surf is a repercussion of that distant turbulence. It seems too bad that the gentle beach must take the abuse when it had nothing to do with the faraway raging winds and rain. But, here again, am I not like the sea? So often the anger and frustration I feel are expressed in the wrong place to the wrong people. How do I handle my anger? Express it, repress it, pretend it doesn't exist? I used to try to hide it. I was so ashamed. I had been taught that a civilized person did not give vent to his or her feelings, but now I realize how wrong that is. Anger is energy. And if it is kept bottled too long, it will finally explode.

Energy must find expression, and anger expressed in a constructive way can be a positive force for good in our lives. Anger repressed for a length of time can turn into violence. Violence against our inner self or violence against someone else, whichever way it takes, becomes a destructive force.

The world has been changed for the better by men and women who have been angry. Angry about life conditions, prejudices, bigotries, the seeming inequities of life—they turned their anger into creative energy. Vaccines were discovered, laws were passed, philosophies were born, schools and charities were established, books were written, and symphonies were composed.

What does this mean to me? It means that even though I am not a Mozart, a Madame Curie, or a Pasteur, I have the power within me to turn my own personal frustrations into creative energy. I can refuse to allow any person or circumstance to diminish me. I can find new ways to solve my problems; I can refuse to let bitterness and resentment eat at my soul until it is old and withered. I can use my anger as a stepping-stone to growth and freedom.

Today I was awake very early and decided to walk on the beach. It was a beautiful morning. The early mist rising from the sea evaporated into the sparkling seashore. As I wandered down the beach, I became so involved in the world around me—the sun, the sea, the gulls, the sandpipers—that for a time the world let go of its hold on me. I became immersed in life, and it came to me that perhaps this is what the experience we call death really is, a time when we let go of the world or the world releases us, when we merge mind, ego, body, and soul into life until that moment when we are ready to begin again. Truly, there is only life, changing, moving life, a series of endings and beginnings. If I look back on what I remember with my conscious mind to the person I was thirty, twenty, or even ten years ago, it is almost like viewing a stranger. How I reacted to life yesterday was from my consciousness of yesterday, how I react today is from my consciousness of today. When I am rehearsing the past, I am robbing myself of now.

Why are we so hard on ourselves? If I had a friend, whom I really cared about, and I knew that friend had made mistakes in the past and had caused pain for himself and others, if I loved my friend would I continually and forevermore shake my finger at him and say, "You're bad, you're guilty, and I will never let you forget"? Oh no, if I loved my friend I would say: "Sure, you made some mistakes; everyone makes mistakes, but they are in the past. Try to learn what you can from them, but remember, my friend, you acted then from where you were at that time; but you are different now, and how you act today is what is important. Forgive yourself, be free, let go, it is past." If I feel this for a friend, then surely I can give the same compassion and understanding to myself.

Soon I must leave Stella Maris and return to the world from which I was retreating. The peace, wholeness, and understanding that I have experienced here by the sea will always be a part of me. I know that when I am again involved with people, work, and things, I will once more have moments of fragmentation and frustration. However, when these times come—and I know they will because the human tides of life ebb and flow as surely as the tides of the sea—to replenish my soul, I will go to that place deep within me—Stella Maris, my retreat, my haven by the sea. I know you understand me because you also have your special place somewhere deep inside of you.

# Notes

1. Charles Fillmore, as quoted in James Dillet Freeman, *The Story of Unity* (Unity Village, Missouri: Unity Books, 2000), p. 54.

2. Francis Gable, "Unity Farm," as published in *Unity News*, July 16, 1927, as quoted in Arthur Zebley, *From the Beginning—Unity, Volume One* (Kearney, Nebraska: Morris Publishing, 1995), p. 137.

3. Furthermore, the practical side to Unity provided a magazine for business people that linked Unity principles and business practices. It was called *Christian Business*, and in 1933 it published its credo.

### A New Business Creed

"I believe in business as a means whereby each member of society may render helpful service to others.

I believe that if any conflict arises between human interests and business, human interest should be placed first.

I believe that the profits of a business should be shared and that this is fundamental to sound business success.

I believe that business, to be of greatest value, must take God into active partnership.

I believe that meditation and prayer are essential to business and personal success.

I believe that business life should be a rich, expanding, abundant life, ever opening new channels of service.

I believe that partnership with God will give a joy, a satisfaction, a faith, and a courage in business that cannot otherwise be obtained."

(This creed is quoted from Arthur Zebley, pp. 174-175.)

4. Marcus Bach, *The World of Serendipity* (Englewood Cliffs, New Jersey: Prentice-Hall, Inc., 1970), p. 72.

5. Krishna, Bhagavad-Gita, as quoted in Marcus Bach, *Major Religions of the World* (New York: Abingdon Press, 1959), p. 28.

6. Some of the best of these columns formed the basis of Lowell's book *The Prayer Way to Health, Wealth, and Happiness* (Unity Village, Missouri: Unity Books, 2000).

7. In his book on the history of Unity, *The Unity Movement: Its Evolution and Spiritual Teachings* (Philadelphia: Templeton Foundation Press, 2002), pp. 95-96, Neal Vahle credits Lowell Fillmore, along with H. Emilie Cady, as being the key force behind Unity's growth.

8. There was a write-up in *Unity News* on April 2, 1928, about Charles and me. I can only presume it happened this way; I was only 2½ at the time!

**Rosemary wears the pants.**
"The scene opens at Rick's home, Unity Farm. Early morning, Charles, age seven,

> and Rosemary, two and one half years of
> age, dressing in the nursery. Loud, con-
> tentious voices float down to the living
> room. Papa Rick calls up, 'What's the mat-
> ter with you kids? Why don't you come
> down to breakfast?' Charles in tears,
> 'Rosemary won't let me have my clothes.'
> Papa Rick, 'Take 'em away from her.'
> Charles, 'I can't. She's got 'em on. She says
> she's a boy and she's going to school in
> my clothes!' "

I'm kidding, but I'm not sure if this alleged incident might
not have shaped my brother's and my future relationship!
(The quote is from Arthur Zebley, p. 143.)

9. I thought a few sample scripts would give a little of
the flavor.

**April 8, 1977**
"The Word"
This is Rosemary Rhea, and the word is *Beginning*!

When the perennial flowers begin to push up through
the cold ground in preparation for their beautiful blossoms, we are reminded of new beginnings. Life does not
begin with birth and end with death, as we commonly
think. A new life can begin at any time with new ideas,
new attitudes, and new ways of solving problems. It has
always been an inspiration to me to think of new beginnings. This means we are not bound to the past. How
many people have you known who learned the art of new

beginnings, and you had to admit, "This is not the same person I used to know"?

"The Word" is brought to you by Unity School. For a free copy of all our thoughts for this month, write APRIL, Box 128, Unity Village, Missouri.

And remember, the word for today is *Beginning*.

## May 12, 1978
"The Word"

... the word is *Learning*!

Any employer of a large number of people will most of the time honestly admit that he or she has made many mistakes. What is more, the employer knows that some of his most valuable employees have made costly mistakes. But this is true in any part of our lives, and the biggest mistake is to begin to fear attempting anything because we might make another mistake. If our minds are open, we learn from mistakes and don't keep making the same one over and over. It is an actual fact that those who don't make mistakes are those who don't ever do anything; but then, that is the biggest mistake of all!...

And remember, the word for today is *Learning*!

## September 11, 1979
"The Word"

... the word is *Balance*!

In caring for ourself and others, it is imperative that we strike a balance. To do that which is for our own pleasure and enjoyment may seem like selfishness to some, but it may also be for our own good health and sense of well-being. Rest and relaxation or just doing something for the fun of it can provide a time for reorganizing our inner resources. Life is to be lived, and it should not be a constant state of sacrifice. While trying not to be selfish, we can remember to care for ourself, respect ourself, and have time for ourself, for this is the balance that brings fulfillment....

And remember, the word is *Balance!*

10. Robert Frost, "Mending Wall," 1914, as quoted in John Bartlett, *Familiar Quotations* (Boston: Little, Brown and Company, 1980), p. 747.

11. Edwin Markham, "Outwitted," ibid., p. 671.

12. Prior to 1963, even the Unity pool was off limits to blacks. David Williamson, who was on staff with the Unity Ministers Association at the time, tells how the Unity pool got integrated:

> "In the summer of 1963 the Y.O.U. (Youth of Unity) was holding a conference at Unity Village. A number of black youths were in attendance. On a hot summer afternoon everyone, black and white, went down to the pool. Only the whites went in for a swim. Blacks stood on the deck watching. Ralph Rhea, the veteran Unity minister who at the time was codirector of the Unity Field Department, happened by the pool. Finding the situation intoler-

able, he hollered, 'Everyone swims.'
The blacks jumped in and from then on
the pool was integrated."
Ralph was like that.
(The quote is from Vahle, pp. 379-380.)

13. Robert Burns, "To a Mouse," as quoted in *The Norton Anthology of English Literature*, Volume 2 (New York: W. W. Norton & Company, 1974), p. 25.

14. Jim Freeman passed away April 9, 2003, shortly after his 91st birthday.

15. Eric Butterworth's *Discover the Power Within You* and *Spiritual Economics* have each sold hundreds of thousands of copies and are considered New Thought classics. Eric made his transition April 17, 2003 at the age of 86.

16. Martha Smock, *Meet It With Faith* (Unity Village, Missouri: Unity Books, 1995).

17. Mary Kupferle made her transition on the same day as Eric Butterworth, April 17, 2003, eight days after James Dillet Freeman. Mary was 87. It feels significant that Unity has lost three of its luminaries all at once, like it's the end of an era.

18. Mrs. Robert Wagner was to the Bel-Air Hotel what Eloise, the everywhere-present and all-knowing little girl from the Kay Thompson children's classic, was to the New York Plaza Hotel.

19. Charles Fillmore, "Reform Your God Thought," as quoted in James Dillet Freeman, *The Story of Unity*, pp. 248-249.

20. James Dillet Freeman, "Life Is a Wonder," *Unity Magazine*, March/April 2002, p. 16.

# About the Author

The granddaughter of Unity cofounders Charles and Myrtle Fillmore, Rosemary Fillmore Rhea was born in 1925, the daughter of W. Rickert Fillmore and Harriet Collins Fillmore. Rosemary says she is the only one ever born at Unity Farm, Unity Village as it is now called.

Rosemary, ordained a Unity minister in 1980, presently splits her time between Unity Village and Jamaica where she actively supports the Unity work in Montego Bay. She also is an active speaker throughout the world, serving as Unity's best ambassador of goodwill.

Rosemary has two children, Rick and Rosalind, to whom this book is dedicated, from her first marriage to Stanley Grace. Rosalind has two sons, Jacob and Adam, from her marriage to Kansas City lawyer Eric Tanner.

Rosemary Rhea began a 25-year career in multimedia in Hollywood, California. Upon her return to Kansas City, she produced and hosted radio station WHB's education talk show *Young Ideas*. After that, she directed and hosted Unity's five-minute television broadcast, "The *Daily Word*," for twelve years. With her late husband,

Ralph Rhea, she initiated the public service program enti-
tled *The Word*, which was on more than one thousand
radio and television stations.

The coproducer of three documentary films, *Around
the World in Search of Faith*; *Charles Fillmore: American
Mystic*; and *Unity, a School of Christianity*, Rosemary has
been listed in *Who's Who of American Women*. She has
been actively involved in the International Relations
Council, American Federation of Television and Radio
Artists, White House Conference for Education for
Missouri, and American Women in Radio and Television
Broadcasting. She presently serves on the Advisory
Council for the Association for Global New Thought.